U0964432

球化背景下教育及英语语言教学

维探究

ultidimensional Probe into Education

LT in the Context of Globalisation

张蓓 著

知识产权出版社
全国百佳图书出版单位

图书在版编目（CIP）数据

全球化背景下教育及英语语言教学多维探究／张蓓著．—北京：知识产权出版社，2017.9

书名原文：A Multidimensional Probe into Education & ELT in the Context of Globalisation

ISBN 978-7-5130-5195-8

Ⅰ．①全…　Ⅱ．①张…　Ⅲ．①英语课—教学研究—中小学　Ⅳ．①G633.412

中国版本图书馆 CIP 数据核字（2017）第 247623 号

责任编辑： 李学军　　**责任出版：** 刘译文

封面设计： 刘　伟

全球化背景下教育及英语语言教学多维探究

张　蓓　著

出版发行：知识产权出版社有限责任公司	网　　址：http：//www.ipph.cn
社　　址：北京市海淀区气象路 50 号院	邮　　编：100081
责编电话：010-82000860 转 8559	责编邮箱：752606025@qq.com
发行电话：010-82000860 转 8101/8102	发行传真：010-82000893/82005070/82000270
印　　刷：北京建宏印刷有限公司	经　　销：各大网上书店、新华书店及相关专业书店
开　　本：880mm×1230mm　1/32	印　　张：8
版　　次：2017 年 9 月第 1 版	印　　次：2017 年 9 月第 1 次印刷
字　　数：225 千字	定　　价：48.00 元

ISBN 978-7-5130-5195-8

序 言

几经周折，在良师益友们热心无私的大力支持下，这本书终于得以出版。写此序言之际，正值2017年高考之际。回首23年前，彼时高考还安排在骄阳似火、挥汗如雨的七月。这二十多年来，高考历经革新完善，时间也人性化地被安排到六月初。光阴荏苒，我也从懵懵懂懂踏进高考考场的妙龄少女步入了不惑之年。高考把我带到了山东大学这个百年老校，之后为了一窥英语发源地之真容，远赴英格兰巴斯大学攻读教育专业硕士学位。毕业回国，怀着满腔的热情走上了高校教育的工作岗位，十几年的课堂教学令我成长、思考，心中有满满的感受，亦存丝丝的困惑，迫不及待地期盼分享与交流。

参加高考至今的23载，跨越了一个千年！进入崭新的21世纪，科学技术的高速发展令人目不暇接，全球一体化进程日新月异。社会结构和经济模式都随之发生了巨大的变化，各国的教育体系也随之悄然变革。世界各国都有自己独特的教育评价体系，这些体系既有相通之处，又符合不同的国情，各具鲜明的特色。在这样复杂多变的背景下，素质教育和评价体系的改革朝向受到各国教育专家们的密切关注，其中测试与评价是素质教育不可或缺又争议不断的课题，评价体系如何指导素质教育的展开，并且对素质教育会产生什么样的影响？从另外一个角度来看，素质教育需要什么样的评价体系与之相匹配？

中国的高考是影响最为广泛和深刻的综合评价选拔体系，又是素质教育和评价体系最具代表意义的交汇之处。本书以此作为切入点，引入西方传统的教育评价理论作为衡量准则，并甄选高考大省山东省的一个应届班级进行个案研究与分析，尝试回答在上一段提出的若干问题。最后，运用“衡量研究方法有效与否的标准”对此研究进行了谨慎评价与适应性分析。同时，对于高考前中小学课程体系设置提出基于本书研究之后的建议。

随着我国经济实力稳健增长，在国际上的地位日益见高。在“一带一路”政策的引导下，越来越多的官方和商业机构都顺应趋势，成立了跨国企业或者在国外设立分支机构。作为多年来国际文化和商务交流沟通的常用语言，英语语言的学习也日益凸显出重要地位。本书的部分章节探讨了英语语言学习的具体问题。

管子曰：“一年之计，莫如树谷；十年之计，莫如树木；终身之计，莫如树人。”在我国这片广袤而丰厚的沃土上，教育阵线的奋斗是一场持久战，既要保持我们五千年的优良传统，又应借鉴西方文明中的长足之处。尤其是在全球化日益深入、信息交换瞬间达成的今天，培养具有更广阔视野的未来栋梁是我们教育行业新时代的神圣使命。

本着为中国教育评价体系的完善和素质教育的持续推进略尽一份绵薄之力的初衷，在无数个寂寂不眠之夜构思、成稿，又几经润色、修改，迟迟未敢付梓，其中缘由，应是对“教育”二字怀有深深的敬畏之心，唯恐立意不高，误人子弟。然而正如丑媳妇还须见公婆，终于在这个绿树成荫的初夏时节定稿，谨奉献给不懈战斗在教育战线的灵魂工程师，见识粗陋，定有诸多不尽完善之处，诚邀指正与赐教。

2017 年 6 月 8 日于泉城济南

PREFACE

In recent years, the turbo-charged development of science and technology has enhanced the process of global integration dramatically. Great changes have taken place in both the social structure and the economic pattern, and the educational institution of each country has shifted accordingly. All countries in the world have their own unique educational evaluation systems. These systems have similarities as well as disparities catering for various national conditions; and each has its own distinctive features. In such a complicated background, the reform orientation of 'quality education' and evaluation system has drawn close attention from educational experts around the world. Assessment and evaluation of 'quality education' remains indispensable and controversial topic in this circle. All these put forward questions like the following,

In what kind of way does evaluation system guide progress of 'quality education'? What is the impact of certain evaluation system on the 'quality of education'?

From another point of view, what kind of evaluation system proves appropriate for 'quality education'?

Chinese National University Entrance Examination is the most comprehensive evaluation and selection system with extensive and profound influence, representing the intersection of 'quality education' and the evaluation system. Taking this as a starting point, selecting a final year class in a senior middle school for a thorough case study, this treatise aims at answering the previous questions according to the western traditional evaluation theory. After analyzing the report result, the significance and generalisation of this research are cautiously evaluated. Finally, recommendations for school curriculum system are proposed based on this investigation.

With the steady growth of economic strength, China's international status increasingly build up these years. Under the guidance of 'The Belt and Road', more and more governmental and business organizations conform to the trend and establish multinational enterprises or set up branches in foreign countries accordingly. As a commonly used language for international cultural and business communication, English language learning is growing in importance. Several parts of this treatise are designed to explore some specific issues involved in English language acquisition.

It's said that education is a life-long cause; the struggle in the education front seems like an endless combat. On this vast and fertile soil of China, education not only involves maintaining our long-lasting traditions of more than five thousand years, but also drawing on the experience from the Western civilization achievements. Especially in this magical age of deepening globalization when information is transmitted within the blink of an eye, it is a demanding mission for us to breed a new generation with broader horizon.

CONTENTS

LIST OF FIGURES

Chapter One

A Proposal Regarding the Introduction of Citizenship Education into National Curriculum

Part I Introduction

Nowadays, it is usual practice that a pair of Thailand-made swim-glasses is purchased by a Japanese who lives in Britain. It is easy for a person who lives in America to enjoy a free chat with a friend at the other end of this globe, say, China, by an exchange delay of usually no more than one second. Numerous such examples could be cited here to illustrate a fact in this changing world, i. e. the phenomenon of what is called the 'global village' by Carpenter and McLunhan (1970: xi quoted by Waters, 2001: 12). In recent decades, with the radical development of computer and information technology, the world is getting smaller in its dimensions both of space and time (Delanty, 2000; Capella, 2000). 'The everyday consciousness is more exposed to events far beyond the parameters of the nation state. These changes in our perception of time and space have transformed the cultural models by which we interpret the world' (Delanty, 2000: 82).

The cooperation among states, the appearance of international economic entities such as the European Community, the common concern on the global environmental issue, the large volume of migration and international exchange of human resources, the convenience of transportation and communication… all of these are indicating a strong tendency of what is called 'globalization' (Waters, 2001). Some argue that globalization is curtailing the power of states and making the border between states fade away. Consequently, the concept of citizenship with a close link with the traditional ideas of patriotism and nationalism are facing a challenge in this changing world (Ichilov, 1998).

Are people losing their distinctive identity as a citizen of a certain state? Is it necessary to introduce citizenship education into a national curriculum? What content should be included within the citizenship education?

This essay aims for trying to answer these questions by an observation of this changing world and on the basis of relevant literature review.

Part II will deal with the changing concept of citizenship within a globalization tendency. Part III will discuss the necessity of introducing citizenship education into a national curriculum and Part Ⅳ will propose a plan of what should be imparted for an appropriate citizenship education.

Part II A Changing Concept of Citizenship Within a Changing World

About the concept of citizenship

Traditionally, the concept of citizenship has a close link with that of patriotism and nationalism. According to Janowitz, the congruence and validity of these three concepts represent attachment and obligation to a country and a political community, in the face of a changing world (Janowitz, 1983 quoted by Ichilov 1998: 13).

Citizenship itself is a complex and multidimensional concept. It consists of legal, culture, social, and political elements, and provides citizens with defined rights and obligations, a sense of identity, and social bonds (Ichilov, 1998: 11). Whereas, Derek Heater has argued that citizenship entails status, loyalty, duties and rights 'not primarily in relation to another human being, but in relation to an abstract concept, the state' (Heater, 1990: 2 quoted by Isin & Wood 1999: 3). He points out that citizenship is one among many identities of an individual, which 'helps to tame the divisive passions of other identities' (Heater, 1990: 184 quoted by Ichilov 1998:11).

'According to Alfred Marshall, citizenship is a status expressing a capacity or competence to be a member of society' (Isin & Wood, 1999: 26). Delanty says that citizenship entails membership of a particular kind of group, namely a political community, involving a set of relationships between rights, duties, participation and identity (2000: 9).

About the concept of globalization

In recent decades, the tendency of globalization with multiple dimensions is advancing to change the pattern of the world as well as the internal structure of states in various aspects.

In general dictionaries, globalization is defined as 'to render global' or 'the act of globalizing' (Waters, 2001: 2).

After some analysis and synthesis of various views about the definition of globalization, Waters gets to the definition as,

> *a social process in which the constraints of geography on economic, political, social and cultural arrangements recede, in which people become increasingly aware that they are receding and in which people act accordingly* (2001: 5).

Delanty says that in sum, he sees globalization as a meeting of cultures as a result of the diminishing importance of space. This can take the form of a violent conflict, the merging of cultures and the formation of a universal culture (2000: 85).

Here I would like to argue that it is the development of science and technology, especially information technology that is impelling the appearance and development of the globalizing process. Science itself is becoming globalized. It has been calculated that there are more scientists working in the world today than have worked in the whole history of science before, and they are in communication with one another much more rapidly than was ever possible previously (Giddens, 2000: 20).

The global integrity of science, technology and economy, the international exchange of human resources and the common concern over environmental problems; all of these clearly indicate the globalizing tendency and thus Held thinks that increasing economic and cultural connections reduce the power and effectiveness of governments at the nation-state level. States have thus been obliged to surrender sovereignty within larger political units and a system of 'global governance' is therefore emerging with its own policy development and administrative systems which further curtails state power, and this provides the basis for the emergence of a supranational state with dominant coercive and legislative power (Held 1991: 207-9 quoted by Waters, 2001: 124). Regarding the right of the state, Waters says that the state might not have disappeared, but it is certainly losing much of its sovereign capacity to control its population (2001: 231).

On the contrary, Yeates indicates that those who argue that globalization erodes the state fail to appreciate that the world political system is still inter-governmental and is premised on constitutionally-sovereign states. Indeed, international cooperation is, at the end of the day, the cooperation of sovereign states. As Drache argues, 'cooperative activity... does not necessarily imply that the cooperating actors somehow fade into the background' (1996:53 quoted by Yeates, 2001: 125). This view accords with that of Delanty: globalization must be seen as an expression of the interaction of different national centres and cultural systems (2000: 84).

Capella holds that globalization means interdependence among nation states (2000: 228). Further more, the concept of 'globalization' implies 'localization' (Waters, 2001: 5). The state lies at the heart of the global governance and invokes domestic politics to explain the content of national social, political and economic reforms (Yeates, 2001: 97). The nation-state is not disappearing or losing its power in the world, but it is being reshaped, especially in the West and especially in Europe. The outcome of this is that, especially in

Europe, we are living in period of fuzzy sovereignty, in which nations are everywhere seeking to redefine their past, and recapture a new identity for the future (Giddens, 2000). I agree on the points that the role of nation-state is changing and adjusting to adapt to the changing world. Whereas, I would like to argue that his emphasis of 'especially in the West and especially in Europe' is not neutral enough. Actually, as a global issue, the process of globalization are almost affecting every state-nation not only the Western countries.

In this widespread and fundamental changing situation, the citizenship concept is changing as well. It is facing the challenge of losing its traditional bearings and calls for new ingredients catering for the new demands.

Changing concept of citizenship within a changing world

The debate over globalization raises the issue of the changing status of the citizen as a member of the nation-state (Amin and Thrift, 1995; Falk, 1994; Held, 1995; Mlinar, 1992; Robertson, 1992; Sassen, 1996 quoted by Isin & Wood, 1999: 156). The existence of 'globalization' redefines the rights and obligations of citizens as members of nation-states (Isin & Wood, 1999: 156). Regarding the global human resource exchange, Isin also points out that especially among the emerging cosmopolitan classes, globalization is undermining the personal attachment to membership in the state (Isin & Wood, 1999: 7).

All in all, the concept of citizenship is experiencing fundamental change in this changing world and is facing a challenge as well. I would like to argue that each state has its own specific characteristics as well as its own identity, no matter how the globalization is booming. In this changing world, a sense of nationality and patriotism related to the concept of citizenship should be strengthened further rather than being weakened.

In my opinion, besides an indication of a person's identity, citizenship is also an orientation that defines what a person is and directs her/his conception as well as behaviour within a certain society and the world. Here I strongly agree with Cogan that citizenship education, in the broadest sense, is an important task in all contemporary societies (1998: 3). The next part will mainly discuss the reasons for introducing citizenship education into a national curriculum.

Part III The Necessity of Introducing Citizenship Education into National Curriculum

Globalization tends to change the world into a 'global village' both in space and time and the borders among states seem to recede. Whereas, I would like to say that it is not possible that people in the world would be unified into the same characteristics due to the difference of history, tradition, custom, culture, etc. Relations among states should be interdependent and cooperative rather than assimilation. Different states have their different situations and particular characteristics. In this rapidly developing and changing world, to set one's standpoint and retain the characteristics of a certain state becomes more significant than ever before.

Citizenship education as an independent subject may or may not be part of a country's national curriculum. The situation in China is complex and interesting since citizenship education is part of the curriculum in some provinces but not in the other. Similar issues are usually dealt with in subjects such as history, geography and ideology education. Nowadays almost all the states are aware of the fact that education is the most potent means of development of the essentials of nationality (Green, 1997). Closely related with the sense of nationality, citizenship education thus is called upon to fulfil this task. As Cappella says that in this changing world, making the power of the vague sovereign explicit is by and large a task of democratic educational institutions (2000: 232). Thus, it is a reasonable argument that the introduction of citizenship education as an independent subject is needed more than ever to provide a sense of purpose, solidarity, and guidance in a fragmented and a rapidly changing world (Pratte, 1988 quoted by Ichilov, 1998: 271).

Part IV Proposed Plan of the Introduction of Citizenship Education into National Curriculum

Aim of citizenship education

Politics is a basic factor in the dimension of citizenship. Issues of political significance arise frequently in subjects such as history, geography and religious education. This serves to remind us, if we needed reminding, that the curriculum is not a neutral thing, somehow extricated from its social and political context (Pearce & Hallgarten, 2000: 14).

Thus citizenship education should basically serve for the interests of the nation. Simultaneously, in this changing world, the contents and patterns of citizenship education will, no doubt, have to be readjusted, in order to adequately prepare the younger generation to assume their role as citizens (Ichilov, 1998: 11). Here I would like to suggest that citizenship education should include the introduction of the changing situation of the world and the specific role of the certain country in the context of globalization.

Different dimensions in citizenship

As has been mentioned in the introduction, citizenship is a multidimensional concept. It is also an indefinite and somehow disputed concept. 'Marshall (1977, 1981) differentiates among three dimensions of citizenship: civil, political and social, and emphasizes the social aspect. The civil element of citizenship is composed of the rights necessary for individual freedom, and the institution most directly associated with it is the rule of law and a system of courts. The political component consists of the right to participate in the exercise or political power. Political rights are associated with parliamentary institutions. Social rights represent the right to the prevailing standard of life and the social heritage of the society. Citizenship in the social sense is based on an individual obligation to contribute taxation to a state system of provision, and to a method of redistribution of resources to those fellow citizens who are unable to provide their own needs. All these forms of citizenship, in Marshall's view, have been institutionalized in the welfare state. The existence of a welfare state is, therefore, 'a requisite or modern democracy and democratic citizenship' (Ichilov, 1998: 11-12).

Basically, citizenship conveys a sense of national identity

combined with relevant rights and obligations, within which the development of the individual, relationships between individuals and relationships between people and the government are dealt with. Another major dimension could be divided into that of patriotism, nationalism, culture and politics.

In my opinion, citizenship education should mainly focus on these aspects. Moreover, a global consciousness should be promoted in this interdependent world. Here I fully agree with those British Global educators on the precepts of 'Think globally, and act locally' in which that the global citizen would be skilled in the arts of peace-making; would have intercultural understanding; would be environmentally aware; would recognize human rights issues, and act on them; and would be able to imagine, and work for, alternative futures (Lister, 1998: 260). Although this still remains disputable within relevant field, this proposal suggests a sound solution for citizenship education in this changing world. In the next section, a proposal of what should be included in the citizenship education syllabus would be discussed regarding to the multidimensional concept of citizenship and the changing situation.

Content proposed to be concluded within the citizenship education

The concept of citizenship contains a sense of the

knowledge, skills, values and dispositions that, ideally, citizens should possess (Cogan, 1998: 2). As citizenship is a multidimensional concept, it would be confusing if there were not one unified conceptual framework in this essay. I would like herewith to adopt the five attributes of citizenship put forward by Cogan to be the main structure and mixed together with the other dimensions mentioned in the previous section. The five attributes are: a sense of identity; the enjoyment of certain rights; the fulfillment of corresponding obligations; participation; and an acceptance of basic societal values (Cogan, 2000: 2). Additionally, I would like to suggest a sixth attribute involving awareness of the globalized situation and the nation's orientation related to this changing world.

a. a sense of identity

A sense of national identity and patriotism is usually seen as an essential ingredient of citizenship (Cogan, 2000: 3). As Heater indicates that citizenship helps to 'tame the divisive passions of other identities' (1990: 184 quoted by Ichilov, 1998: 11), conveying to each individual citizen a society's collective memory; cultural togetherness and nationality and the collaborative sense of purpose in fraternity (Ichilov, 1998: 11).

In China, for example, the unflagging support for respect for labor and the collective, as well as patriotism and loyalty to the Communist Party, constitute an enduring theme in the content of moral education (Lo and Si-wai, 1996: xix).

b. rights

To be a citizen is to be a member of a group and thus to be entitled to the benefits that group membership confers (Cogan, 2000: 3).

Marshall has argued that in the Western world, citizenship rights can be classified into three categories: legal rights; political rights; economic and social rights (Marshall quoted by Cogan, 2000: 3). This summary of citizenship rights does not only apply to the Western states, but also well fit for almost all the democratic states. Students should be fully aware of the rights they are endowed as citizens of a certain nation.

c. obligations

In many Western democracies, there is a trend among citizens to claim their rights and to retreat into their own privacy. However, a neglect of the community, of the national public place as well as of the international public space results in the loss of the sense of trust, efficacy and neighborliness. There are rising levels of crime and violence, homeless people, racism, social inequality, abuse of the environment, violations of human rights, etc. , which all pose problems, nationally and internationally (Ichilov, 1998: 271).

Capella argues that it is not possible for someone to have a right if no one has a duty to match that right. He says that when one asks specifically about the content of the rights of citizenship, it is the same as asking who has the duties corresponding to those of citizenship (2000: 232).

As rights guarantee a citizen's freedom, the obligations act as restraint which helps to confine people's behaviour into its rightful scope. It is universally accepted that citizenship carries with it the obligation to perform certain duties, including the responsibility to obey the law, to pay one's taxes, to respect the rights of other people, to fight for one's country and generally to fulfil one's social obligations (Cogan, 2000: 4).

Janowitz (1983) assigns special significance to obligations on the part of citizens—i. e. , the contributions and sacrifices a citizen makes to keep the political system effective—for the viability of democracy. Citizens must be motivated to perform their duties willingly. In this respect, he considers citizenship to be closely linked with patriotism and nationalism because the latter provides an incentive to fulfill civic obligations. Janowitz defines patriotism as 'a sentiment of belonging; a sense of identification similar to religious, racial, or ethnic identifications. It has been historically associated with the ethos of modern national societies' (1983: 8 quoted by Ichilov, 1998:14).

d. participation

Capella mentions two spheres in the concept of citizenship, i. e. private sphere and public sphere. The private sphere is the world of qualities and particularities: thus, each person's religion, race, cultural qualifications, and sexual orientation; the public sphere is the realm of common affairs in each modern society as such, in the established society. It is, factually or potentially, the relevant sphere for everyone (Capella, 2000: 231). Thus, part of the problem of the definition of citizenship education was that there were at least two views: the passive citizen view-training for conformity and obedience; and educating the future citizen for active participation in a democratic society (Lawton, 2000: 11).

In the active participation respect, I appreciate the concepts of 'a good person' and 'a good citizen' suggested by Cogan: a good person lives his or her life virtuously and honourably, but without any involvement or interest in public affairs. A good citizen, by contrast, not only lives decently in his or her private life, but is also committed to participation in public life; at the very least to taking an informed interest in public affairs and, ideally, playing an active part in them (2000: 4). Thus, by the introducing of the two concepts, Cogan makes the point that participation is what makes 'a citizen' distinguished from only 'a person'. He puts emphasis on active participation in social affairs rather than only obeying all the obligations passively. Some commentators even insist that the most pressing obligation of all for a citizen is participation in public affairs (Cogan, 2000: 4). For example, in Japan, citizenship education programmes tend to emphasize the concept of 'nation' more than that of 'citizen'. Moral aspects of citizenship are nearly always included in the concept of being a 'good citizen' (Cogan, 2000: 6).

Boulding thinks that citizenship education should help to redefine the public place, and to create conscientious, efficacious, interested, caring, and active citizens. Youngsters must be made aware that the 'public place is not only physical space… it is social space… [it] is action space, where we can tend to the arrangements that enhance our mutual well-being as society' (Boulding, 1988 quoted by Ichilov, 1998: 272). Pearce and Hallgarten also agree that citizenship education should equip individuals for active engagement with the social and political lives of their communities (2000: 14).

e. acceptance of basic societal values

It is not possible that one could live without others. People make up that what is called society and the state. They cooperate and interact to survive and develop. In this process, the rights and obligations related to the concept of citizenship help to manage and smooth relations among people. Within a certain society, it is necessary for citizens to be ready and able to decide for themselves while at the same time respecting the viewpoints, interests and rights of others (Cogan, 2000: 5). The concept of 'deliberative citizenship' is held by some commentators, arguing that citizens must be able to think, to reflect, to discuss and to act in ways that are rational, reasonable and ethically defensible (Cohen, 1989; Mathews, 1996; Miller, 1993 quoted by Cogan, 2000: 5).

In this sense, this attribute is a further step of the participation in the social affairs.

f. global awareness

The demands of national citizenship should not be denied, but must be combined with a realization that no nation can operate in isolation in today's world, so that citizenship must contain both national and multinational dimension (Boulding, 1990; Commission on Global Governance, 1995; Ramphal, 1991; World Commission on Environment and Development, 1987 quoted by Cogan, 2000: 5).

I agree with Ichilov that it is evident that present-day societies are highly diverse, and are becoming increasingly more ethnically, nationally and racially heterogeneous, more regionally fragmented, more pluralistic culturally, and more strongly linked with global affairs. Citizenship education limited to inculcation of traditional patriotism or conventional nationalist ideology is obviously insufficient in a highly dynamic, complex and interdependent world (Ichilov, 1998: 268). Therefore, citizenship education should also promote global awareness, and the realization that circumstances that affect our immediate moral and physical well-being are located in the transnational arena as well. Many objectives which should affect the quality of life of each citizen on the planet cannot be accomplished without global awareness and cooperation (Ichilov, 1998: 273). To find out the balance between citizenship education and globalization tendency will ease up the tense that exits between them.

Part V Conclusion

In this essay, aiming at promoting the introduction of citizenship education into national curriculum, discussion about the concept of the citizenship, the concept of the globalization and what should be introduced as the content of citizenship education are dealt with respectively in Part 2, 3 and 4.

Basically, citizenship education is a national issue, serving the mutual interest of the whole political community. It is closely related to politics. I would like to argue that citizenship education should be based on the relevant items set in the national constitution. Thus, a citizenship education could not be seen from a neutral view. It often reflects the interests of those in power in a particular society and thus has been a matter of indoctrination and the establishment of ideological hegemony rather than of education (Apple, 1979, 1982; Bourdieu and Passeron, 1977; Snyders, 1976; Whitty, 1985 quoted by Cogan, 2000: 6).

In the past, citizenship education has not been introduced into the national curriculum as an independent subject.

Nowadays, in the rapid development of globalization situation, preparing the younger generation for their citizenship role is a formidable objective in our kaleidoscopic and rapid changing world (Ichilov, 1998: 267). It is necessary to introduce citizenship education into schools which is expected to give the young citizens a sense of identity, and often of national pride; and to teach them the rights and duties of citizenship as officially defined (Cogan, 2000: 6) as well as inculcating in the younger generation citizenship competences which embrace a profusion of qualities of intellect. These enable the individual to collaborate fully in the enterprise of creating and sustaining a viable and healthy democracy (Porter, 1996 quoted by Ichilov, 1998: 271).

Citizenship itself is a complicated and multidimensional concept. Summarizing from various relevant literature, in Part 4, I introduced the five attributes which are mainly proposed by Cogan to demonstrate what should be involved in school citizenship education. I would like to say that the basic point should be the rights and obligations and their interdependence. All the other dimensions interweave and interact with each other in the multidimensional concept of citizenship.

Although some argue that the development of globalization tends to assimilate the states, I prefer to agree that the relationship between states is interdependence and cooperation rather than assimilation. Within this context, it is more important for citizens to have a sense of national identity rather than losing it. Additionally, an awareness of the globalization and the changing world should be an inevitable part of citizenship education.

It has been observed that lots of states are searching for their way of citizenship education at present to meet the requirement of the changing context. I would like to argue that there will never be a definite and perfect syllabus for citizenship education since the world will never stop changing. Citizenship education should always be updated and readjusted to matching the ceaseless change.

Chapter Two

A Probe into Chinese NUEE and its Impact on Education

This chapter is committed to offer some advice for the prospective curriculum reform in China proposed by the State Department for the continued enhancement of 'Quality Education', which aims at cultivating students' creativity and aptitude. Focused on the National University Entrance Examination, taking the 'diploma disease' as a literature base, I carried out research into perceptions of the National University Entrance Examination (for the sake of concision, I will use 'NUEE' or 'the Examination' to address the National University Entrance Examination in the following parts of this book) and the correlated education with a 50-student final year class of a provincial senior middle school. Data collection was mainly done through questionnaires and interviews. The research findings reveal that students are aware of limitations in the education they experience and the 'backwash' effect of the NUEE on this education system. They appear to accept the necessity of the examination but suggest a broadening in its scope and in the university selection process, introducing new criteria for selection that emphasize a more complete education. The research results show that the students want the courses to be more practical, to be more closely related with real life. The class with whom the research was carried is not portrayed as being necessarily 'typical', but it is still maintained that valuable lessons could be learned from their views toward their own educational experiences.

This research gains particular value from its coincidence with new curriculum reform in China. By analyzing the objectives of education, the correlation between assessment and learning improvement, the correlation between assessment and curriculum, and analyzing the research results, some advice is suggested in this report for curriculum reform of foundation education. The main courses I recommend are citizenship education; psychological education; individual financial management; finance; economics and music. Among these courses, citizenship education will be highlighted. The necessity and suggested content of taking citizenship education are illustrated in relevant part.

Part I Introduction

For many years, the National University Entrance Examination has played a vital role in Chinese educational circles and has had a profound influence in the whole society. When a child enters primary school, or even into kindergarten, s/he begins her/his preparation for this unified examination. Like sprinting in a race, senior middle school students undoubtedly face the direct pressure. In China, it is a tradition for senior middle school students to try their best to succeed in this examination. This impact, or 'backwash' of the Examination on the whole of the education system shows a tendency of what is called the 'diploma disease' by Dore (1997).

Before 2003, the NUEE was regulated to be held on 7, 8 and 9 of July; it was jokingly called 'Dark July' for the attendees. In China, July is the hottest season and not pleasant for strained exams. In 2002, it was changed to be held on the 7th and 8th of June by the State Department. Instead of 'Dark July', a new name appeared to describe the importance of these two days and the days before and after—it is 'NUEE festival'.

As in most countries, the National University Entrance Examination draws much attention from various social classes as well as various areas. Much has been addressed in the literature about the general policy on the Examination and about how to succeed in it. However, little has been done about the specific opinions of the attendees towards this Examination and the backwash of the NUEE on students' learning improvement.

As a summative exam for middle school and primary school, the NUEE reflects the guidelines and the educational goals of the government. Fortunately, this excessive burden on students, especially on the senior middle school students, has been noticed by key people in education circles. The government is consistently keeping on searching for an appropriate balance between the Examination and the 'Quality Education'. The concept of 'Quality Education' has been proposed by Chinese Education Department. In the past, much emphasis has been put on the academic performance of the students but little on other factors, whereas, society calls for people with full-scaled aptitude such as good physical and psychological functioning, other than only good academic marks. Thus, the 'Quality Education' aimed at fostering all-round-ability students is advocated in recent years. Correspondingly, Chinese education has experienced some reforms after the establishment of People's Republic of China in 1949. At present, the National Education Department is planning a reform of the middle school and primary school curriculum and this programme is planned to be put into effect in the coming years. The focus of this reform is mainly the improvement of the 'Quality Education'. The details are now undergoing research and discussion. What is examined decides what is taught in school (Lowe, 2003). Curriculum and assessment cannot be separated. If the curriculum is reformed, the NUEE and relevant assessment system must be reformed correspondingly to fit with the new curriculum and the updated reform aim.

In the preparing and experiment of curriculum reform, there is much of "what teachers think"; "How teachers feel"; "What the experts think"; and "How the experts feel". But I think, as the principal part of the learning process, the students are also of the same and even more significant. I want to know "What the students think" and "How the students feel". From this point of view, I aim to generate something useful for the process of curriculum reform. Since it is the final year students in senior middle school who are facing the NUEE, and they have experienced all the middle school and primary school schooling, I would like to focus on them to help me in this research.

Is the National University Entrance Examination really

so important to every one as it appears to be? Is university study the most beneficial investment for life? Should the senior middle school study focus mainly on how to deal with the National University Entrance Examination and play the game well or on students' learning and aptitude improvement? In the new circumstance of globalization and rapid development, what kind of schooling can meet the requirements of bringing up qualified citizens to serve our country? When I think about the NUEE, these questions always come into my mind and concern me a lot. Empirical research is driven by research questions (Punch, 2001: 34). As the beginning step of a research design, the principal task is to identify a practical topic, or we should say, a research central question which is academically focused, constructive and answerable (Poulson & Wallace eds. , 2003). I will introduce my research question as well as the subsidiary questions which generates the whole design. All these questions above could be combined into this question:

What is the impact of the National University Entrance Examination on students' learning improvement and what are the implications of this impact for educational reform?

It is this question that impels me to carry out the research addressed in this book. This research will mainly be focused on these following subsidiary questions:

a. Why do students want to take the NUEE and go to university?

b. What do students do to prepare for the Examination?

c. What are the students' opinions about the Examination and learning?

d. What do students think that they have got from their schooling and what do they expect to get from their schooling?

e. What subject do students want to take?

By doing this research, I am trying to obtain a relatively clear conception about the particular situation of the students who are facing the NUEE. Furthermore, I hope that the relevant policy makers will pay more attention to the positive elements of the assessment for students' learning improvement, trying to avoid the development of the potential 'diploma disease' (Dore, 1997).

Part II Literature Review

1. What 'diploma disease' is and its relation with the research questions

'Diploma disease' was initially put forward as a notion by Dore in 1976 in his book by the name of *The Diploma Disease: Education, Qualification and Development.* Twenty years later, i. e. 1997, the problem of 'diploma disease' was dealt with as a special issue in the journal *Assessment in Education: Principle, Policy & Practice.* With the development of globalization in various orientations, the trail of the 'diploma disease' which appeared in 1970's has grown and expanded rather than being cured. 'Diploma disease' is like 'inflation', or 'economic stagnation' of the (mutually interacting) unintended consequences of what Dore has called a 'process common to all societies' (Dore, 1997: ix). This concept could also be interpreted by another phrase brought up by Dore, 'qualification escalation', indicating a steady rise in the qualifications required for any specific job, also known as 'qualification inflation', which means a steady fall in the job-getting value of any particular level of qualification, leading to people staying on in school longer than either their intrinsic person-development benefits from learning or their need to learn something occupationally useful would justify (Dore, 1997: ix).

I would like to argue that the 'diploma disease' is a social issue rather then only an educational problem. It is the actual social situation that acts as the guideline for educational policy-making and educational orientation. As an essential part of education, assessment undoubtedly is influenced by social factors (Broadfoot, 1996).

It is not difficult to see that contemporary society is awash with various tests. It is usual practice that a certain position will require certification and testing. In more and more intense competition, the requirements are climbing higher and demanding higher standards. It is not surprising that a position only requiring a senior middle school graduate is competed for by hundreds of candidates with master's degrees. As a backwash to the schooling, it is becoming common for students not to consider work until they have achieved a master's degree. These years, the candidates who take the Graduate Entrance Examination proliferate at an amazing speed. Correspondingly, the quota for entrance keeps enlarged year by year. More and more graduates with higher and higher certification are 'produced'. The labour market is becoming more and more competitive, especially for graduates. Such being the case, the students are facing heavier pressure. As Dore indicates:

> *Schools used to be for educating people, for developing minds and characters. Today, as jobs depend more and more on certificates, degrees and diplomas, aims and motives are changing. Schooling has become more and more a ritualized process of qualification-earning (1997: back cover).*

I agree with Dore that the 'diploma disease' is derived from the growth of modern bureaucratic organizations which 'rationalize' their recruitment processes by using educational records—particularly performance in general education subjects—in order to identify suitable recruits (1997: ix). This bureaucratization of recruitment methods is likely to generate the problems of misallocation of social resources and the degradation of the teaching-learning process (Dore, 1997: ix).

What Dore says about what he calls 'diploma disease' describes a general phenomenon prevailing in contemporary society in China. As Dore has said, it is common processes to modern societies (1997: viii). Like 'inflation', or 'economic stagnation', the value of academic certifications has been depreciated during employment competition.

Through research conducted with the final year students in a senior middle school, my research questions involve two basic words, 'why' and 'what' centered on the educational assessment.

'Why should people learn?'

'What should people learn?'

To connect them with assessment, these questions thus could be developed into 'should people learn only for the purpose of succeeding in assessment and getting certification?'; 'Should people learn for the sake of learning or for doing a job or for getting a job?'

To put these questions further, I would like to examine and discuss the structure of the subjects which are offered for students and assessed in the NUEE to see whether they are really necessary and whether other subjects should come into the current curriculum.

2. The objectives of education

When talking about educational issues, I would like to argue that the objectives of education should not be ignored. Why do people educate and get educated? Various answers have been given to this question.

Here I would like to agree with Butterfield that

> *it is difficult to attempt to address all the possible meanings of the term 'objectives ' at once. On the one*

hand, there are objectives of policy makers for the education system itself; on the other, there are more specific learning objectives that teachers and students might be working to in particular lessons or sequences of lessons (1995:9).

Dore says that *education is supposed to civilize people, improve the quality of life (Dore, 1997: 26).*

In China, It is generally accepted that education is a kind of social activity that trains people. The activity of education itself is inseparable from the development of society and the development of individuals. The objectives of education are to: help people with the gaining of knowledge and skills; influence and perfect people's morality and value concepts; train people into qualified individuals who are helpful for the particular society (Education chapter in Great Chinese Educational Encyclopaedia, 1985: 172 quoted by Hu et al. , 2000: 161).

Hu points out that many countries take the national educational objectives as: cultivating people who are physically and psychologically healthy and harmoniously developed (Hu et al. , 2000: 453).

I agree with Broadfoot (1996) that education is basically a social concern. It is closely connected with politics and the development aim of a particular country. From this point of view, I conclude that the principal objective of education is:

producing qualified citizens for the country. By qualified citizens, I mean citizens who are healthy and independent, with the capabilities of surviving and developing in the society.

The proposal of the concept of 'Quality Education' is a measurement to achieve this purpose. The education system in the past was not adequate to meet the new changing circumstances. 'Quality Education' aims at cultivating people with practical capabilities and innovative creative spirit rather than only achieving a good mark in rote-learning; gaining an overall development in the aspects of ideology, culture, body, mental, labour, etc. (He, 2001: 474).

3. Brief introduction to the Chinese National University Entrance Examination

It is said that China was the first country to introduce an assessment system for the selection of civil servants in the Sui Dynasty. It was reformed and improved in Tang, developed in Song, Yuan, Ming, and finally come to an end in the Qing Dynasty (Tou, 2004).

Having prospered for hundreds of years, the Imperial Examination had its own advantages at certain times, setting up some fundamental, influential but not always beneficial ideas in China. For instance, the Imperial Examination advocated that schooling is the best and the only way to succeed in one's life. Nothing is more nobler than taking the Imperial Examination and succeeding in it to be a government officer. With the world development, however, this assessment system hindered the political and economic development of latter-day China.

In 1949, the People's Republic of China was established. Meanwhile, the educational assessment system was reformed to meet the requirements of the new national circumstances. In 1977, after the 10-year Cultural Revolution, the *People's Daily* announced that a unified national university entrance examination would be restored (Lewin, 1997: 140). In 1978, the National University Entrance returned to act as the major legitimate means to select outstanding students into universities.

> *Entrance examinations were reintroduced in December 1977; the principles of selection have become again the rigorously meritocratic, elitist, educational achievement norms that were overthrown, presumably once and for all, by the youthful activists of the Cultural Revolution.*
>
> *(Passin, 1978, 319-320 quoted by Dore, 1997:197)*

At that time, the government paid for the university students for almost all of their cost. withal, the government was responsible for the allocation of a job to university graduates. To some extent, this meant that entering the university was a guarantee of an official job.

In the following years, higher education has been gradually moving away from direct government control. The 1993 'Outline' gives more power to universities to determine student enrolments, decide specialities offered, and change organizational structures. Central government will only maintain close relations with a core of key universities. Others will be free to operate admissions policies that they themselves define. The outline also made it clear that:

> *The proportion of students sponsored or self supported will be gradually increased... The government will no longer pay all the expenses of college students and a fee system will be gradually introduced. Higher education is non-compulsory so students should be principle pay tuition and other costs themselves. Loan programmes will be launched to help students from disadvantaged families... The old system under which every graduate was guaranteed a job will be replaced by one in which only a small number of graduates will be assigned jobs by government with the majority finding employment by themselves... Only graduates who major in Education and others who study specialities which involve work in harsh conditions and who come from remote area will be assigned jobs (SEC, 1993: 29 quoted*

by Lewin, 1997:152).

From then on, the take-in quota of universities was enlarged every year and the university entrance rate to the students who sit the Examination became higher and higher. In 1994, the higher education take-in ratio for NUEE is 46. 7 percent. In 2004, it is 73. 2 percent (Proposal of the Improvement of the Educational Structure, 2004).

However, the tendency of the 'diploma disease' impels students to seek for further education after graduation from university. Relevant research in recent years shows that the burden on students grows heavier rather than lighter as expected. The differences between universities urge students to compete as severely as before. Despite these situations and enthusiasm in succeeding the NUEE, a consideration of the advocation of 'Quality Education' has been generated and is being explored. Meanwhile, the world is experiencing a dramatic developing and changing stage. The generation of new technology, the advancement of science, the boost of omindirectional globalization... all of these call for an updating of our national education system. Regarding this, the problem of the curriculum setup in middle school and primary school has become a key issue in recent years. The National Education Department is brewing a reform of the curriculum. Correspondingly, the NUEE would be reformed simultaneously.

4. The correlation between curriculum and assessment

a. The importance of curriculum setup

The National Education Council points out that, the essential mission of the educational reform is enhancing the 'Quality Education' both significantly and across the whole system. In the process of the implementation of the 'Quality Education', the core issue is the setup of a new curriculum for foundation education which fits the new requirements (Jiang, 2001: 1).

The content of curriculum is the embodiment of the content of schooling. By the curriculum, the national educational guideline is carried through, the training purpose of the schools is realized, and the instruction for the students is processed. If the composition and content of the curriculum has problems, the schooling will come out with problems as a result. From this point of view, the problem of curriculum is a central feature of schooling (Jiang, 2001: 1; Butterfield, 1995; Hu et al. , 2000; Zhang, 2001).

In recent decades, society, science and technology are experiencing rapid development. The whole world is undergoing dramatic transformation. School education should be reformed to catch up with these development and transformation. The school curriculum should be reformed as a result. It is because of this that many countries have made and are making educational reforms. And, the reform of the foundation school curriculum is taken as the core task or essential task (Jiang, 2001: 1).

b. The function of assessment

Assessment is a very significant and substantial part of school education. Promoting children's learning is a principal aim of schools. Assessment lies at the heart of this process. It can provide a framework in which educational objectives may be set and pupils' progress charted and expressed. It can yield a basis for planning the next steps in response to children's needs… it should be an integral part of the educational process, continually providing both "feedback" and "feedforward". It therefore needs to be incorporated systematically into teaching strategies and practices at all levels.

Assessment is an indispensable part of education and plays an important role in improving teaching and learning. Meanwhile, as an effective measuring tool, assessment is used in social selection for access to higher position or better opportunity. As society is becoming more and more complex, differentiated and bureaucratic, a variety of forms of assessment are applied in a wider and deeper extent within our everyday life. The influence of its social and managerial role is getting more prominent and crucial. Have the social and managerial functions of assessment increasingly displaced educational functions? This section will aim at analyzing the difference and correlation between these two main functions of assessment in relation to my own experience and social circumstance and tries to make it clear how we could apply these two functions appropriately in social and educational practice.

Broadfoot says,

> *Assessment is a central feature of social life. Passing judgment on people, on things, on ideas, on values is part of the process of making sense of reality and where we stand in any given situation. Even very small children can make assessments...*
>
> *(Broadfoot 1996:3)*

This statement on assessment provides us a general idea about what assessment is and shows how assessments are widely spread in our social life.

Most of us, especially people in China, have the common feeling that assessment seemed an everlasting theme while we were at school. Since it is so important to assess and be assessed, what are we doing it for? Here are some descriptions about the functions of assessment from different sources:

Bloom, Hastings and Madaus (1971)

I. Diagnostic:

II. Formative:

III. Summative:

And Gipps and Stobart (1990):

I. Professional:

II. Managerial:

III. Mixed:

And the third one, Broadfoot (1996):

A sociological analysis of functions

I. Certification:

II. Selection:

III. Control:

Little indicates that the roles of assessment are: for formative feedback on learning; for summative evaluation; for the monitoring of standards; for certification; for selection (Little, 1997: 5).

These educational professionals have their own very views towards the functions of assessment. These points look different since they consider it from different perspectives. Nevertheless, it is possible for us to make a general conclusion out of these, that is:

Basically, assessment has two roles to play: an academic role and a social role. For the academic role, assessment serves for formative feedback and summative feedback, enhancing learners' learning improvement by providing information about the learning process. Whereas, assessment is also employed for the social purpose of selection and control. It is hard to say which of them is of the more importance. What really matters is how to achieve an appropriate balance between them.

As a summative assessment of middle school and primary school education, NUEE exerts both of the functions at the same time. It reflects the quality and result of the foundation education. At the same time, it decides the selection into higher education and further study.

It is also important to remember that many assessments explicitly or implicitly embody a number of social, emotional and physical characteristics of students. Thus an assortment of behavioural, attitudinal, socioeconomic, cultural and family characteristics often constitutes a 'social diagnosis' in accounting for students' failure to make satisfactory progress or fulfil their potential. The work of teacher, school and educational districts are, in turn, also 'assessed' by governments and their agents, by parents and local communities, employers, the media and so on. Educational assessment contains many social factors and will interact with society. In this sense, besides its educational functions, school assessment also comprises social and managerial functions.

Essentially, education is a social product and a social issue. The social circumstance and requirement determine the education system and its content. It is inconceivable to imagine that we have an education system which has nothing to do with our society. Many of the educational assessments perform a managerial function simultaneously.

An analysis of developments in educational assessment procedures reveals more clearly than perhaps any other aspect of the education system the irreconcilable demands which education must fulfil in contemporary society. From the outset assessment procedures were a crucial part of the process of opening up routes to social mobility and the institution of a more rational basis for the allocation of social roles. On the other hand, it is important to recognize the role of assessment in limiting such mobility and, even more crucially, in legitimating what are essentially still education systems strongly biased in favour of traditional privilege. For this reason and as a result of new social and economic imperatives, recent decades in many developed countries have witnessed growing discussion with many traditional forms of assessment.

Assessment should be a powerful tool for learning, not merely a political solution to perceived problems over standards and accountability. In order to raise the standards of attainment of individual pupils further the important contribution of everyday teacher assessment in planning for progression throughout the key stage needs to the recognized and development.

c. The correlation between curriculum and assessment

As it is described, assessment is used to evaluate what the learner has attained from his or her learning process and how well he or she performs within this certain attainment. This can both be formative and summative, giving feedback to all the people involved in the learning and affecting the future learning at the same time. In this way, assessment performs an educational function, especially in schools.

Assessment is so important in school education not only because of its functions of supplying feedback; what makes it more important is its functions in enhancing the teaching and learning process. This point could be shown in the following diagram:

Diagram 1

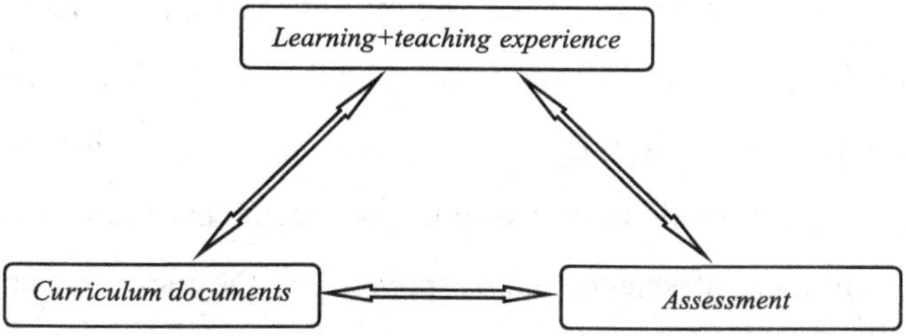

(Lowe, 2003)

This diagram indicates that learning and teaching experiences are realized and influenced by the curriculum documents and the assessment process. What is assessed decides what is taught and learned. For the realization of the implementation of the 'Quality Education', a matching assessment and examination system must be set up first. *The Compendium for Curriculum Reform of Foundation Education (Draft)* indicates explicitly that the assessment system reform is one of the objectives of the curriculum reform. Moreover, the *Compendium* has proposed the guideline for assessment system reform. This shows that the assessment system is not only a guarantee for the implementation of curriculum reform; it is one of the significant parts of the curriculum itself (Research Group of Curriculum Reform, 2003: 6).

The NUEE determines what is taught and learned in middle school and primary school, especially in the senior middle school. The University Entrance Examination in China has been tested and reformed and improved in recent years. In Shandong, the NUEE takes the module of '3+X' (different provinces and districts take different modules). Generally, students are divided into two cohorts—students of humanities and students of science. Correspondingly, they are examined for different subjects. All together, they have four units (3+X) to take. The '3' are Chinese and foreign language (students can choose one of the following six freely: English, Russian, Japanese, French, German and Spanish) and mathematics. For mathematics, there are two different examination papers for humanities students and science students respectively. The 'X' unit is also different for them. The humanities students take a comprehensive humanities unit (including history, geography and politics) and the science students take a comprehensive science unit (including physics, chemistry and biology).

As indicated by Diagram 1, assessment has a backwash effect on the curriculum and influences the learning and teaching practice, and so the curriculum of the senior middle school is set up mainly surrounding these subjects. It is a central concern of this book that backwash from the current form of the NUEE is likely to inhibit the attempts to introduce 'Quality Education' to some extent. Therefore, an analysis of the impact of NUEE is indispensable for proposing suggestions for curriculum reform.

Part III Methodology

Regarding the definition and purpose of research, quite a few experts have contribute their own opinions,

McNiff points out that research is about creating new knowledge, finding ways of testing its validity, and sharing the knowledge for a specific purpose (McNiff et al. , 2003: Part 1). Leedy defines it from a more utilitarian point of view: research is a procedure by which we attempt to find systematically, and with the support of demonstrable fact, the answer to a question or the resolution of a problem (Leedy, 1989:5 quoted by Walliman, 2001:7). Kerlinger uses more technical language to define it as: the systematic, empirical and critical investigation of hypothetical propositions about presumed relations among nature phenomena (Kerlinger, 1970:8 quoted by Walliman, 2001:7).

They define ‘research’ from different aspects but share common ideas in their views. All of them emphasise the *special purpose,* with which we deal as the research question in a specific research task. Another word worth noticing here is *systematic* or its adverb form *systematically*, this word is mentioned almost in all of these quotations and indicates a systematically planned *endeavour* or *procedure* aiming at that *special purpose* involving in a research.

Thus, a conclusion might be deduced here from all the above mentioned that the systematically planned procedure is of the utmost importance for a research which is aimed at answering a specific question. When conducting a research study, how to plan, or we use the word *design,* it will influence the answer to the research question which will come out as the result of the process.

McNiff thinks that the research design *may be understood as the overall plan. It explains how the research will be conducted (*McNiff et al. , 2003:10*).* Whereas, Punch says that the main function of research design is that it *connects the research questions to data.* He makes this concept more specific as *basic plan for a piece of research*, and he states four main ideas of a research design: strategy, conceptual framework, the question of who or what will be studied and the tools and procedures to be used for collecting and analyzing empirical materials (Punch, 2001:66).

It can be inferred from these two ideas to say that research design is an overall plan which connects the research questions to data centred on those four main ideas. So may I modestly suggest here that the important thing for a research design is to generate a good plan of data collection and data analysis to be connected closely with the research question and answer the research question as well as possible. With this understanding, I would like to state how I will plan my investigation to answer the research question in this report. Before proceeding to the next part, I would like to reintroduce my research question here again, that is:

What is the impact of the National University Entrance Examination on students' learning improvement and what are the implications of this impact for educational reform?

And the subsidiary questions are:

a. Why do students want to take the NUEE and go to university?

b. What do students do to prepare for the Examination?

c. What are the students' opinions about the examination and learning?

d. What do students think that they have got from their schooling and what do they expect to get from their schooling?

e. What subject do students want to take?

1. Style of research

I choose to do this research in Shandong Province, China, in my hometown. Since my research is focused on the National University Entrance Examination, and it is the final year students who take the Examination this June that are facing these questions directly, I plan to focus my research in a specific class in Grade 3, the final year students in a provincial senior middle school.

It is not appropriate for me to go to a senior middle school class for this research since these students concerned had an extremely tight schedule every day, although fieldwork will provide me more detailed and first-handed materials; and unfortunately I have to abandon a very useful tool for research, that is, observation; but I believe that painstakingly designed and conducted questionnaire and interview processes after the NUEE would make up for this deficiency to some degree.

Considering my current situation, I prefer a case study for this research. As Bell points out that the case-study approach is particularly appropriate for individual researchers because it gives an opportunity for one aspect of a problem to be studied in some depth within a limited time scale (1991: 6). The great advantage of a case study is that it allows the researcher to concentrate on a specific instance or situation and to identify, or attempt to identify, the various interactive processes at work (Bell, 1991: 6).

Besides these strengths, a case study has its own weakness. Since it is only a research of single event, generalization from it seems impossible and the value of the study remains to be questioned (Bell, 1991: 6). However, Bassey indicates that case studies are valid forms of educational research if they are carried out systematically and critically; aimed at the improvement of education; relatable; and they can, by publication of the findings, extend the boundaries of existing knowledge (1981: 86 quoted by Bell, 1991: 6).

2. Data collection methods adopted

a. Brief introduction of my strategy in planning the methodology

A relevant literature review on the topic of my research question should be the first step in the research design. It makes a sound basis for the next step taken in a research.

As has been mentioned above, I will choose a specific class from the final year of senior middle school. First, a questionnaire will be given to every one of the class for them to fill out. After careful analysis of the responses, I will choose six students from them for a further detailed interview focused on the research questions.

Since this research style is a case study, I am actually interested in getting into something deeper to find an answer rather than taking a wide-ranged survey to come up with a statistical analysis. I would like to put more emphasis on interviewing six students. The questionnaire serves as a complementary method. Here some differences between interview and questionnaire help me to decide this strategy.

Interview has more opportunity for probing and generating new constructive questions (Cohen & Manion, 1989: 292). I appreciate this advantage of interview to satisfy my research purpose set in this book. Whereas, interview has its own limitation, typically, the number of respondents who can be reached is limited (Cohen & Manion, 1989: 292). A questionnaire approach which is designed to reach all of my target population is a good solution to this weakness of interview. Although the information got from a questionnaire is relatively superficial, it does help in offering a general understanding about the whole class. Cohen says that the questionnaire return rate is often poor (1989). I think it really depends on specific situation. In a large survey targeting a great number of a population, especially when this survey is conducted by mail, there really exists a worry about the return rate. But in my research, which is a case study focused on a particular class, I could moderately estimate the questionnaire return rate could be at least above 90 percent.

In this sense, the method of interview and questionnaire will work their own ways as well as mutually benefit in my analysis of data collection.

One useful feature of closed-ended items in particular is the uniformity that they build into questionnaire responses, which allows for relatively easy quantification and reliability.

However, questionnaires can also be customized, not only to obtain highly detailed and individualized information, but also with the purpose of truly involving participants in the process of data collection and analysis so as to make use of their insights. An example of a data elicitation procedure of this nature is a grid-based scheme, which a researcher can create following the analysis of a completed questionnaire and after carrying out an in-depth interview with a participant. The grid is designed both to reflect the participant's input, as well as to uncover further information, including the participant's perceptions about the patterns and relationships in the data collected to date (Gass & Mackey: 2011:166).

b. The language I propose to use in questionnaire and interview

When I am designing the questionnaire and interview questions, it is a little difficult for me to decide which language to use. English is convenient for me to apply the results to my report directly. However, I could not expect thorough and fully-expressed responses from my interviewees whose first language is not English. Since the quality of reliability is very important for a research, I decide to sacrifice convenience for the sake of reliability. I will design the questionnaire and interview in both Chinese and English and ask my respondents to give me the answer in either of the languages as they prefer. This may add more work for my research proceeding, however comparing with what I would get from it, I believe it is worth doing.

c. Relevant literature data collected from library and website

This kind of method is a secondary data collection. From library and the internet, I can get relevant information related to my research questions, as presented in the previous chapter.

d. Questionnaire

Closely relating its content to my research questions, I draft a questionnaire for students with two parts, involving questions about the students' attitudes to NUEE, attitude to school learning and the current school assessment situation. These questions involve both fact-gathering and attitude-type scaling task (Punch, 2001). I design different types of questions for different tasks. The first part is composed by open questions and the second part mainly consists of close questions. Open question allows students freedom to express their opinions, but it is relatively difficult to analyze. Whereas, close question is much easier to analyze and conclude. At the same time, it reduces respondents' freedom of response. To suit the type of data I expect, I choose a mixture of them to form this questionnaire. Additionally, analysis of open-ended questions is not such difficult a problem in a small-scale study.

In the process of questionnaire drafting, I always bear in mind that a questionnaire should be attractive to look, brief, easy to understand, and reasonably quick to complete (Munn et al. , 1999:21). The piloting work will be done with my colleagues and I will also ask them for feedback and comment. The idea is to help me practically in checking and modifying the draft.

When the questionnaire is completed, I will email it to my friend Tao, a senior middle school teacher, for him to print out and distribute to the target class. I will ask him to distribute envelopes along with the questionnaire and asked the students to seal the completed questionnaire to ensure its anonymity, an advantage which few other research techniques could offer (Munn et al. , 1999: 4). This point is very important in this case study in that facing the stressing NUEE, some of the students are inevitably getting a little nervous for a variety of reasons. If they feel that they do not want others to know some of their personal opinions, it would be possible that I could not get the most genuine responses which I need; and this would have a negative effect on my research result. Therefore, offering an appropriate way of keeping students anonymous is a necessary measure.

Tao will collect the completed questionnaires, and then send them to me.

e. Interview

When I receive the completed questionnaires, I will analyze them before the interviews are conducted. The analysis result will be a part of the answer for the research questions. And also, it is a pilot study for the interview questions design and modification. From the students' feedbacks, I could get some new ideas and fresh perceptions regarding the actual situation in the class which would help me to modify and adjust my original interview design to be more specific, focused and clearly-oriented. I plan to use a structured interview, one in which the content and procedures are organized in advance (Cohen & Manion, 1989:293). Although a structured interview allows little space for flexibility and new-idea-generating, this kind of pre-scheduled and closely-structured interview is suitable for my research to get the most information related with my research questions within a limited period of time.

Almost all of the students have convenient access to the internet. This enables me to conduct the work easily. After choosing my interviewees, I will contact them by email, getting familiar with them, introducing my interview purpose and sending them my proposed interview questions before hand. Then we will use WeChat as the communication tool for interviews. This is a little different from face-to-face interview; but it is the best possible way I could manage to initiate at present. It will lack the body language and facial expression which might denote some additional information; however, it spares the strangers' embarrassment as well. It seems that people tend to feel safer and be comfortable to tell what they think at ease through the internet. Unlike face-to-face and telephone interview, it gives more freedom for a second thought and there is more 'wait time' for the interviewee to fully develop her or his ideas. The 'depth' is what I appreciate the most in this interview. Additionally, it is easy to save the interview conversation on my laptop to keep a complete and accurate record, hereby enhancing reliability.

3. Sampling

As the basis of all research, the method of sampling is undoubtedly crucial for any research and its outcome (Gorard, 2001) (Munn et al. , 1999). The sampling issue is usually a tricky one since it is not easy to find an appropriate balance between the target population and the chosen sample in the design to reach the best result of both accuracy and generalization in a research. However, as my research set in this report is a case study, it is not so hard a task to make a decision on sampling. My target population is a final year class in a provincial senior middle school with 50 students. I will use questionnaire and interview as the main method to accomplish this research task.

a. Questionnaire sampling design

The questionnaire sampling will involve all the students in the class. *If the numbers involved allow you to cover the whole of your target population rather than just a sample, then it is always worthwhile to do so (Munn et al. 1999:17).* This one hundred percent sampling would fill in the margin of uncertainty and make it relatively 'unbiased sampling' (Munn et al. 1999).

It is important to remember, however, that this class does not necessarily constitute a sample that is representative of the wider student population, so that results cannot be generalized to that wider population.

b. Interview sampling design

Compared with a questionnaire, an interview approach is designed to deal with problems in the aspect of depth rather than breadth. It is not necessary and also not practical to interview all the target population. Sticking to the principle of minimizing the margin of uncertainty and trying to make a relatively 'unbiased sampling', which helps to minimize the possible inaccuracy of the research generalization, I plan to use a stratified sample to cater for the purpose of the 'representative' sample (Munn et al. , 1999:17) of the target class. To put it into detail, I am going to interview six students from the class. These six students are chosen after a stratification according to their academic performance. Two of them are from top 10 and two from medium and two from the last 10. Firstly, I will divide the whole class into 3 groups according to their latest academic performance ranking. Then, divide each group into girls and boys cohorts. Thus, I got six cohorts altogether. Choosing one from one cohort randomly makes up the 6 interviewees.

This approach cannot represent all of my target population since every one holds her or his own opinions toward the same issue. But by this stratified sampling, I am trying to maximize the degree of generalization function of the sample.

Still like the questionnaire, the interview will be conducted anonymously and I will give them fictitious name in this report to preserve their personal rights. I will tell them about this before interviews start.

Part IV Chronology

<table>
<tr><th colspan="3">Tasks</th><th>Time</th><th>Remark</th></tr>
<tr><td colspan="3">Research design</td><td>06 May 2014</td><td></td></tr>
<tr><td rowspan="5">Questionnaire design</td><td colspan="2">Draft</td><td>10 May 2014</td><td></td></tr>
<tr><td colspan="2">Pilot</td><td>12 May 2014</td><td></td></tr>
<tr><td colspan="2">Check with colleagues and finalizing</td><td>16 May 2014</td><td></td></tr>
<tr><td colspan="2">Hand out</td><td>17 May 2014</td><td></td></tr>
<tr><td colspan="2">Collect</td><td>01 June 2014</td><td></td></tr>
<tr><td rowspan="9">Interview questions design</td><td colspan="2">Draft on the basis of the feedback of the questionnaire</td><td>03 June 2014</td><td></td></tr>
<tr><td colspan="2">Pilot</td><td>05 June 2014</td><td></td></tr>
<tr><td colspan="2">Check with colleagues and finalize</td><td>06 June 2014</td><td></td></tr>
<tr><td rowspan="6">Interview</td><td>Wang (M)</td><td>25 June 2014</td><td>On internet for 4 hours</td></tr>
<tr><td>Jin (F)</td><td>26 June 2014</td><td>On telephone for 1 hour</td></tr>
<tr><td>Liang (M)</td><td>26 June 2014</td><td>On telephone for 45 minutes</td></tr>
<tr><td>Gao (M)</td><td>29 June 2014</td><td>On telephone for 1 hour and a half</td></tr>
<tr><td>Yu (F)</td><td>2 July 2014</td><td>On telephone for 45 minutes</td></tr>
<tr><td>Lu (F)</td><td>2 July 2014</td><td>On telephone for 45 minutes</td></tr>
</table>

Part V Data Presentation

1. Feedback of Questionnaire

This research is conducted in a final year class in senior middle school. There are 50 students altogether, with 24 females and 26 males. They are between 18 and 19 years old. Their average age is 18. Fifty copies of the questionnaire are handed out and 50 copies of answered questionnaires are collected. This means that the feedback rate reaches 100 percent. However, some of the items of some the collected copies are left blank.

The questionnaire is produced in both English and Chinese. It is stated clearly that they could answer the questions in either of these two languages. Five of them are answered in English and others in Chinese.

a. Part 1 of questionnaire

There are eight open questions in the first part of the questionnaire.

The first question is 'why do you want to go to

university?' Most of the students answer that they want to learn knowledge for self-development and therefore get a good future career and life. The number of the students who give this answer is 48, occupying 96 percent of the whole class. Four students answer that they want to go to university to take further study for making a better contribution to our country. Four say that because every one wants to go to university. Two think that going to study at university is what they desire the most, they want to realize it. And one says that she wants to repay her parents by entering university. Because this is an open question, some students give more than one reason. Thus I get more than 50 answers. The same case applies to some of the other questions in this part.

The second question is 'What major would you like to study at university?' There are many kinds of answers for it, including almost all the current majors available at university. They are: space science, computer science, mechanism engineering, education, medicine, chemistry, law, electronic and electronical engineering, information technology, oriental philosophy, biology, business administration, economics, business, management, foreign languages, computer engineering, programming, environmental science, ecology science, music, fine arts, internet, food science, etc.

Majority of the males prefer engineering and computer science; there are 13 students out of the total number of 24, more than 50 percent. Twelve girls want to choose medicine, but no boys; that is a large proportion, nearly 50 percent of the 26 girls.

Besides these various and interesting answers, there are 11 students who have not given a clear answer. They say that they have not made a decision on it. It depends on the specific situation. They are willing to choose their major according to their interests and also take the prospect of the major itself into consideration. That means they pay attention to the demands of the society and want to choose a major which will give them great opportunity in the future job seeking.

The third question is 'What's your plan after graduation from University?' Thirty students say that they want to go to work. It is of 60 percent of the whole class. Among these 30 students, as an echo to the second question, 12 girls say that they want to be doctor. Besides going to work, 10 say that they will go on for postgraduate study (20 percent); Five answer that they want to do their own business, say, set up their own company; One says he wants to get married after graduation from university and 1 says he wants to go abroad for a further study. Like the second question, there are 3 students who answer that they cannot make a decision at this time. It depends on the specific situation when they graduate.

The next question is 'What will you do if you fail the NUEE?'

Nineteen of them say that they will take another year's study and sit the NUEE one more time, nearly 40 percent of the class. Among this 19, 14 of them are female. Five answer that they do not know what to do if they fail the Examination because they think they must succeed in NUEE this year. Eleven students say that they will look for a job if they fail to go to university. One of them adds that he does not think that it is a shame to go to work without going to university. Eight of these 11 are males. There are also 5 students who say that they will try to do their own business if they cannot go to university. Four say that they have no specific idea about this question. Three say that they will look for other chances of schooling, say technological training or studying abroad. And two answer that they will teach themselves. Another student just leaves this question blank.

The fifth question is that 'Are the tests results and ranks made public each time? If yes, what's your opinion about it?'

For the first part of this question, fifty students answer 'yes' as expected, because it is a tradition in Chinese schools. The focus of this question is on the second part—the students' opinion toward this. Four students say that they have got used to it since it has been like this since they entered school and they just feel indifferent about it. Thirty-six students reply that they agree with it. Almost all of them give the reason that it helps one to get a clear conception of one's own learning achievement and the difference with others. They think that this is good for a positive competition and motivates them to study harder. They occupy 72 percent of the class. Whereas, 20 percent, 10 students give the opposite answer against it. They say that they do not like the tests results and the ranks made public because it makes one lose face and feel discouraged. A student adds to say that the academic results only reflect one aspect of people's capability; but he also admits that it is really hard to find an optimum way which can reflect the overall performance of capability.

The sixth question is 'What are the most important things that you think you have gained from your schooling?' Thirty-three of them say that they have learned knowledge, learning methods and skills from their 12-year school. This accounts for 66 percent. Twelve (24 percent) answer that schooling helps them learn to be good persons. Ten say that the most important thing they get from school is friendship and the art of getting along with other people. Two say that schooling prepares them for all-round capability. Two say that they learn to be useful citizens for our country and society. Two say that the most important thing they have got from schooling is the perfection of moral character. One student says that he thinks the most important thing he has learned is the method of getting to know the world.

The seventh question is 'Have your teachers been

teaching you exam skills? Do you think them useful?' All of the students say that they have been taught exam skills. Fourty-five students (90 percent) hold that the exam skills are useful. They agree that exam skills offer a good strategy for answering the questions, as well as help them avoiding unnecessary errors and maintaining a good psychological state. Nevertheless, one student agrees with this but also says that he thinks the exam skills are useful for exams, but not practical for life. And 6 out of the 45 students say that the skills are useful to some degree, but they are not decisive factors, what really matters is still the actual strength, that is, the students' actual capability of acquiring of knowledge and capabilities. Another 5 students say that the exam skills are utterly of no use.

The eighth question is 'Do you think it reasonable that the admission to university is determined by the result of NUEE? What other factors do you think should be counted in the university entrance selection process?' This is also a productive question and I get abundant kinds of answers. Some think it is rational because every thing has its strength as well as weakness. NUEE is an acceptable way for the main selection means of entrance to university. Above 70 percent of the students think that it is not perfect. The suggested factors should be considered are:

Sociality, practical ability, all-round capabilities, daily

performance in the school and the daily academic results, ability of analyzing and dealing with specific tasks, participation in social activities, moral character, awareness of teamwork, physical making, survival skills, and the enthusiasm for one's speciality.

Some suggest that an interview after the NUEE should be included into the university entrance selection. Some suggest that some of the extra bonuses to the NUEE results (this will be further explained in presentation of the ninth question of the interview part) are not reasonable and should be cancelled. Some think that it is unfair that the 'admission marks' for different provinces are different and Shandong Province often gets the highest admission marks. They suggest that all the candidates in China should share the same standard.

b. Part 2 of questionnaire

The second part of this questionnaire involves eleven questions.

The first question is about students' opinion to the NUEE. 'How important is NUEE to your life?' The answer can be shown by Diagram 2,

Diagram 2

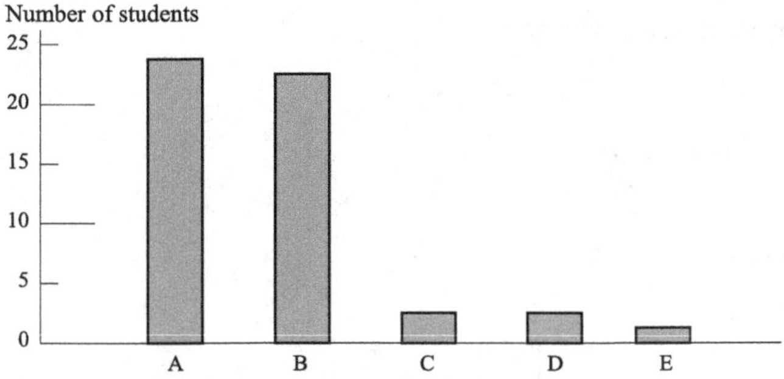

A=very important; B=important; C=indifferent;
D=not important; E=hard to tell

This diagram shows that 90 percent, that is 45 students think that NUEE is significant to them. Twenty-three students out of them think that NUEE is very important and 22 think that it is important. Two feel indifferent to it and 2 think it not important. Only 1 student cannot decide how to give a clear answer.

The second question is about the students' confidence of success in the Examination, 33 students answer that they believe they will get a satisfactory mark in NUEE. One thinks that he has no confidence and 16 tick the 'hard to tell' choice.

The next question is 'Do you plan to take the NUEE again in case you fail it this year?'

For this question, the replies come out with a half to half result. Fifty percent of the class want to take the NUEE in the next year and 50 percent will not. Among the 25 students who want to sit the Examination again, 14 are female and 11 are male.

The fourth question is 'Do you feel that your current study is intense?' The proportions of different choices are demonstrated in diagram 3:

Diagram 3

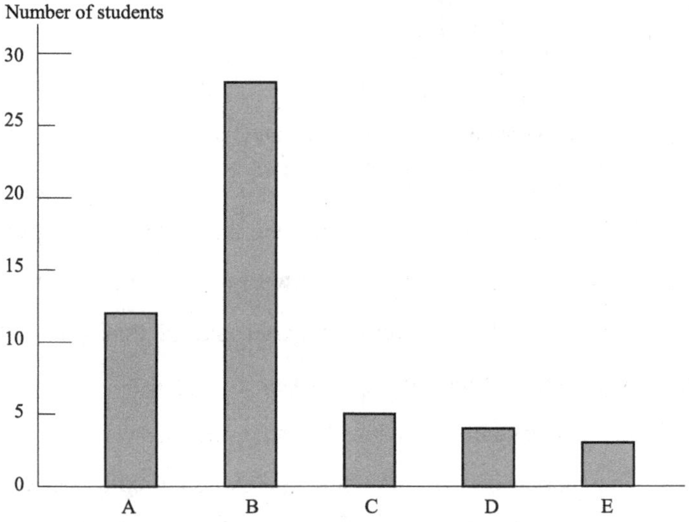

A= extremely intense; B=very intense; C=fairly intense; D=somewhat not intense; E=not intense at all

The choice of 'B' scores the highest as indicated in Diagram 3. Twenly-eight students think that the study before the NUEE is very intense. And 12 students think that it is extremely intense. Five feel it is fairly intense and 3 think it not intense and 2 just find it not intense at all.

The fifth question asks the student if they have mock exams for NUEE. All of them tick the 'yes' choice. The sixth question is a further approach of the fifth, asking about the frequency of the mock exams. All of the students give the same answer 'dense'. And one student adds that about twice a month. The seventh question asks about students feeling toward the frequency of the mock exams. Twenty-nine students think that it is a little too much, 58 percent of the class. Thirteen students think it appropriate, about 26 percent. Twelve percent, that is, 6 students think it too much. Two students think it a little infrequent and no one thinks the mock exams are too few.

The next question asks that 'Do you think mock exams helpful?' Ninety-four percent students say 'yes' and only 6 percent think it of no use.

The ninth question is about students' opinion toward exams. The results are shown in Diagram 4:

Diagram 4

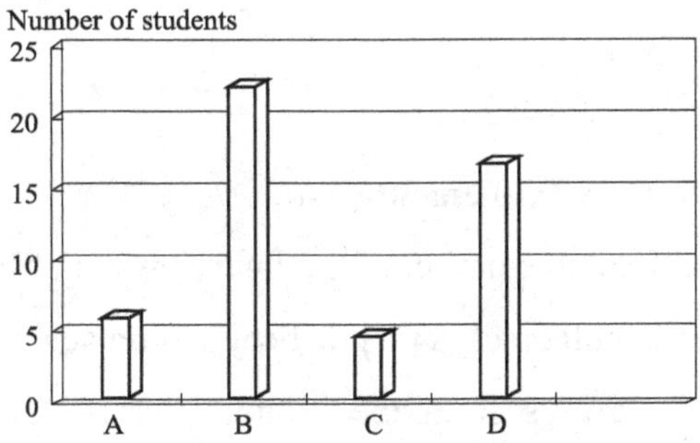

A=yes, I like the exams; B=no, I do not like exams
C=I feel afraid of the exams; D=I feel indifferent

Column B is the highest one here. It represents 22 students, 44 percent of the class. They do not like exams. The next is D, 34 percent, means 17 students feel indifferent to exams. six students say they like exams and 5 just feel afraid of exams.

Question 10, 'How many hours do you spend on studying yesterday?' Two students leave this item blank. Two say that they cannot remember it exactly. The most one is 24, which is impossible; and the least is 2 hours. After all, most of the students have spent approximately 10 hours per day on study.

The last question asks about student's interests and hobbies after school. It turns out that the students have a wide range of interests. Most of the girls like reading, listening to music, drawing, and walking and the boys intend to like kinds of sports, especially basketball and football. A high portion of students enjoy surfing the internet, accounting for about 65 percent.

c. Interview Implementation

Actual implementation of the interviews is influenced by questionnaire outcomes and practical circumstances, and in some details differs from the original design. This part is about the influence of the questionnaire outcomes on the interview implementation.

When I get the feedback of the questionnaire, I do a brief analysis on them and use this to generate the questions for the interview in consultation with my colleagues. Here I would like to explain one thing about the questionnaire. When I am working on the questionnaire draft, one of my colleagues suggests adding a note at the end, encouraging the students who feel they have something to comment on the relevant issues to volunteer to take part in the interview. Since I find out from their class director that there are not big differences in academic performance among the students in the class, I decide this is a good way to get those who are ready to help and really have something to say. Thus, I add the note as shown at the end of the questionnaire (Appendix 1). Fortunately, I get 9 email addresses and 1 telephone number, 4 girls and 6 boys. I choose 6 of them, 3 girls and 3 boys to do the interview.

Firstly, I get in touch with my interviewees by email and inform them what I am going to do and how they can help me with it, explaining the objective of my research and enquiring if they would like to help me to take a further conversation. The time is after the NUEE and the students are considering their choice of university application according to their NUEE marks. I only get two replies unfortunately. They are Mr. Wang and Mr. Liang. (To preserve anonymity, I address them by fictitious name in this book.) Thus I contact with their class director to select 4 students who are willing to do the interview with me according to the stratified principles I have stated in the questionnaire sampling part of the methodology section. They are Miss Jin, Miss Yu, Miss Lu and Mr. Gao. Therefore, I have 6 interviewees to go on with this research.

2. Interview results

The first interview is with Mr. Wang. The interview is carried on WeChat through internet as I have proposed in the research methodology design. The result is interesting. It turns out that it is not a structured interview as has been expected, though semi-structured instead. Because it is of a written form, I cannot help getting new ideas from his reply. It lasts for more than 4 hours for two sessions separately in the morning and evening. When I ask what subject he thinks he would like to take but the school has not offered, I proceed to ask what subject he does not like. He says he likes physics and chemistry and does not like mathematics. I ask what about his academic performance of these three subjects. He says mathematics and physics are not satisfying but chemistry is good. I ask why he likes physics and yet the result is not good. And so on… this makes 10 more questions beyond the original question. Although they are not utterly of no use, it really goes a little farer away from the topic and takes too much time. Thus, the next interview with Miss Jin is on the telephone, taking 1 hour altogether. It proves to be a more productive one and the next 4 are all carried out through telephone. The first internet interview is saved on my laptop and the other 5 are recorded by dictaphone and transcribed.

Before stating the interview result, I would like to introduce these 6 students briefly. Mr. Wang and Mr. Liang reply to my email for an interview. Others are recommended by their class director. Miss Jin and Miss Yu are top ten students. Mr. Gao is of medium level and Miss Lu is usually listed in the last 10. Whereas, one thing should be mentioned here is that this class is in the key senior middle school in Shandong Province, one of the best schools, above 80 percent of the graduate students can go to university. There are few students who are really not good at studying and who do not want to go to university.

All of the interviews are done in Chinese. This makes us communicate well with no difficulties and unexpected misunderstandings. In the presentation, I would like to summarize the 6 students' replies question by question.

The first question is 'Do you think that the knowledge you are now learning at school is useful and practical for your future career? If yes, to what kind of degree? '

Mr. Wang says that he thinks what he is learning at school is of not much use for his future career. Whereas, Miss Jin sees this question in a different way. She thinks that she wants to be a doctor and the chemistry is useful for her further study at university and the profession after university. Other subjects perhaps have no direct relations with what will be learned at university and the future profession, but they can offer some good ideas for life and work. She cites the physics and mathematics as examples in that physics helps to explain daily phenomena and mathematics offers a person ways of logical thinking. Mr. Liang says that Chinese and English are important because language is a tool of communication. He adds that communication is of utmost importance in society; but he does not like mathematics. The final year of the senior middle school has some part of advanced mathematics such as differential calculus. He thinks it too difficult and has no practical use. He wants to take a job related with finance after graduation from university. But there is no subject about finance and economics before university. Mr. Gao says that Chinese, English, and a part of mathematics are useful for him. But he does not like chemistry and physics. He explains that if one does not take chemistry or physics as a speciality at university, these two subjects are completely useless. He himself will not. Miss Lu wants to study electronic engineering. She thinks that mathematics, physics and chemistry are useful; but politics is of no use.

The second question is 'Do you think that the subjects which are examined for NUEE are rational? What other subjects do you think necessary to be taken?' All of the six students think that the subjects which are examined for NUEE are reasonable and acceptable as a whole. Whereas, they propose some new ideas separately for the second part of this question. Mr. Wang thinks that psychological education is necessary, because students are at the ages of growing up. Psychological health is important for them. Especially for the senior middle school students facing the NUEE who have some psychological pressure, it will really help. Miss Jin also agrees that psychological education is necessary from the very beginning of schooling. She says she wants to take a course about personal finance. She receives money from elders every Chinese New Year and pocket money from parents. She wants to take a course which can teach her how to manage this money better. Additionally, she says that she thinks it will be better if the subjects are designed to be more practical and have more relations with everyday life. Moreover, she plans to choose economics to study at university, but she feels regret that there is no subject about economics before university. Mr. Liang takes great interests in music. He has practiced trumpet for 6 years. But there is only a music course once a week in the first Grade of senior middle school and it is too easy for him. He wants to take something to a much deeper degree which really helps him to learn something useful. Mr. Gao thinks that the existing subjects are satisfying and he has nothing new to comment on it. Miss Yu thinks that a course of individual character perfection will be useful. Like Mr. Liang, Miss Lu also thinks that she would like a course of music. Besides, she wants to take a course of computer science because she has interests in it.

The next question is about the fourth question in the first part of the questionnaire, some answer to go on with studying in case of failing the NUEE, and how and where to go on with studying? The choices expressed by the interviewees include colleges run by local people, colleges taught by correspondence, vocational colleges, taking another year study for NUEE, going abroad for study, learning practical skills for survival, etc.

The fourth question is 'For the fifth question in the first part of the Questionnaire, the majority of the classmates answer that they accept the exam result be made public, because it helps to know one's learning achievement and the difference from others. Additionally, this helps positive competition and making progress. However, if you are free to choose whether the exam result be made public or not, what will you choose and why?'

Answers for this question are unexpected. From the questionnaire, I get the idea that students have got used to the situation because it is that case. So in the interview, I develop this question by asking if they have the freedom to choose, what they would prefer. Surprisingly, all of the interviewees want the exam result made public. The reasons are the same as those stated in the questionnaire. Only Mr. Liang recommends as a possible alternative that the exam results and the ranking be sent to students individually instead of posted publicly. He thinks this helps to save face for the students who have not got a satisfactory result and ranking, and also helps students to have a clear concept of their academic performance.

Questions 5 to 10 are about the eighth question in the first part of the questionnaire, which asks 'Do you think it reasonable that the admission to university is determined by the result of NUEE? What other factors do you think should be counted in the university entrance selection process?' I get productive results for this question as has been cited in the previous part of the feedback of the questionnaire. These resourceful answers provoke me to ask further explanations about it.

The fifth question is 'For the eighth question in the first part of the Questionnaire, many classmates mentioned that the moral character, civics, and the ability in taking part in social activity should be taken into consideration for the university selection, do you agree with this and what do you think about it?'

Mr. Wang strongly agrees with this idea. He also gives a negative example to prove that it is very important. He takes the example of Mr. Haiyang Liu who poured vitriol on a bear in a zoo cage to have a research generated for his own interests. This case aroused great attentions from the whole society. People felt shocked about the ignorance of Mr. Liu, who was a registered student of Tsinghua University, one of the best universities in China. Mr. Wang adds that Mr. Haiyang Liu is far from being a qualified university student. People like him should not be admitted into university because he has not got a healthy moral character and a sense of the existence of the whole society. Miss Jin also agrees that this is reasonable for the consideration of admission into the university. She emphasises participation in social activities. She thinks that it is of great significance; it helps to cultivate a sense of being one of the members of a society.

Mr. Liang also strongly agrees on this point. He says that he thinks the objective of education is to bring up people who are beneficial for themselves and beneficial for the society; who are responsible for themselves; who are able to get along well with others and society. Thus, moral character is an inevitable part of education and should be considered into the criteria of university admission. Additionally, Mr. Liang mentions about the assessment system for moral character. He tells me that there exists an evaluation for students' moral character and participation in social activities, such things like this besides academic results. This evaluation will be put into a student's personal dossier and it will be a lifelong record.

Nevertheless, the university admission seldom considers this aspect. He also says something which can partly explain the reason why the moral character of students weighs so little; it is the evaluation system for moral character itself. He says that it is only a routine to finish. Beyond achieving a high score in the NUEE, teachers pay little attention to moral character evaluation and seldom care about students in this aspect. He wants a specific, all-round and individual evaluation. He thinks that this will verily help students to improve.

Mr. Gao highlights the participation in social activities. He says he wants to do it, but the school seldom offers this kind of chances. In his memory, there is only one time that he and his classmates went out to sell flowers on Valentine's Day.

Miss Yu also agrees with the idea proposed in the question. She says that every one is a member of society. People need to cooperate with each other for surviving and developing. The awareness and capability of teamwork is of the utmost importance. Perfection of moral character and participation in social activities should be an essential part of education.

Miss Lu agrees that the moral character should be considered for university admission and also mentions the evaluation system of this as Mr. Liang says.

Closely linked with this question, the next question is

about citizenship education. When being asked about citizenship education, all of my interviewees answer that they have never heard about it and have not had such a subject at school. Thus beyond the question itself, I briefly explain the objectives of citizenship education and six possible aspects of citizenship education which I have proposed in one of my essays for the MA in education. After listening to my explanation, all of them strongly agree with it. They think it is very important and necessary. If there is a course like this, they are willing to take it. Mr. Wang tells me that politics which is held in junior middle school and grade one of senior middle school contains something like this but not specific, therefore has little practical meaning. Others agree with this. Mr. Wang says that nowadays, getting along well with others is important. He would prefer a course which teaches how to deal with the relationship between individuals and the relationships between individual and the society. He thinks this is a basic factor of being a good citizen. When talking about patriotism in citizenship education, Miss Yu says that although school education contains something about patriotism education, she does not think that it has done a good job. She tells me that Chinese scenery sites which are listed in the World Heritage rank at third place in the world. She herself is very proud of being Chinese. However, she finds that her friends do not love our country as much as she thinks they should. She adds that they worship the western system and western things randomly. And some of them only know studying hard for a high score in examination, caring little about society and their orientation in society. Mr. Liang has a more specific idea regarding this topic. He says that the love for our country is something too big to describe. He thinks patriotism could be embodied in daily behaviour, including love for one's family, love for one's class, love for environment, etc.

The seventh question is 'For the eighth question in the first part of the Questionnaire, some mentioned unifying the minimum entry score of the whole country, what do you think about this?' Only Miss Yu agrees with the unification. In opposition, Miss Lu thinks that unification of the admission mark is not rational. Others feel indifferent about it. Mr. Wang thinks that it is not possible to realize at least in ten years since China is so widely-stretched and the difference between districts are great. There exist big gaps and various situations. Unification of the university admission mark can not serve to solve problems.

The eighth question is 'For the eighth question in the first part of the Questionnaire, some mentioned adding an entry interview into the university entrance selection process, what do you think about this?'

Miss Lu is the only one who opposes this suggestion. All

five other interviewees agree with it. They hope that a chance for interview could be given in the university admission. Whereas, all of them express their worries about the practical operation of this within the existing situation. Miss Jin points out directly that she is afraid that it will generate unfair cases which are likely to fail good students to give way for some one who has some other ignoble advantages beyond the candidate's quality itself.

The next question is about the extra score added to the examination results for university selection. This includes offspring of overseas Chinese, offspring of servicemen, offspring of martyrs, and students with a certificate of master sportsman.

For this question, I do not get a clear answer from all my interviewees. All of them agree that not all of the items are reasonable and part of them should be cancelled. But the talks with them show that it is difficult for them to tell which one they agree on and which one they are opposed to.

The tenth question is 'For the eighth question in the first part of the Questionnaire, some mentioned taking the daily performance in school into consideration in the process of university entrance selection other than the sheer one-off NUEE, what do you think about this?'

All of the students say that they think it is reasonable and fair. To sum up their ideas, they think that it helps to evaluate students more completely. Miss Jin also proposes to set up an academic points system which summarizes students' academic results of each semester and combines them to contribute a certain percentage to the final score for university selection. In other words, she suggests that the score for university selection should be composed of daily academic results as well as NUEE results.

The next question asks students to talk more about the examination skills.

Students recognize the rationality of examination skills in different degrees.

Mr. Wang says that there are lots of skills, including ticking a choice randomly in case you do not know the answer at all instead of just leaving it blank. But he still believes that what really matters is what you really have learned and a good psychological state. These are the actual guarantee of getting a good examination result.

Miss Jin says that the examination skills are very important. It can help one to do one's best in the examination, avoiding misunderstanding of the items.

Mr. Liang says it is not useful for every one. However, he does not think the examination skills which are taught by teachers are utterly useless. It provides a sort of method in gaining a better result in examination.

Mr. Gao thinks that the skills are fairly helpful in

examinations; but not so helpful in knowledge learning.

Miss Yu thinks that the examination and learning are of the same importance and examination skills are good for her.

Miss Lu understands that examination skills are a product of 'Examination-Oriented Education' ('Yingshi Jiaoyu', some educational professionals say that education in China is 'Examination-Oriented Education' which emphasises too much on Examinations, thus in some degree, ignoring learning itself.). By learning the skills, she can understand the assessing purpose of the examined items, that is, the purpose of the person who designs the examination. This can avoid unexpected misunderstandings.

The twelfth question is a further question of the eleventh, asking the students about the correlation between examination and learning improvement.

Mr. Wang says that the examination helps one to know one's strong point as well as weakness to improve learning. Miss Jin says that the examination is especially useful for the subjects which you take little interest in. Examination offers motivations by its pressure on you. Mr. Liang agrees with Miss Jin on this point. However, he still thinks that too much pressure will have negative effect. Mr. Gao says that examination is a necessary method of assessing one's learning progress. He also agrees with Mr. Liang on the negative effect. Besides stating all the above, Miss Yu suggests that the examination paper should be closely related to reality, focusing on explaining, analyzing and solving practical problems. She says she thinks practical capabilities are the most important thing for her.

The next question is about the opinion the students hold toward the importance of diplomas. Mr. Wang does not think he cannot live without diplomas but he believes that diploma can help him to lead a better life in the society. Miss Jin says that getting a satisfactory diploma is a necessary qualification for getting a good job. Others think similarly. Miss Lu also highlights that what she thinks really matters is still one's actual capability which will support one during one's life besides getting a diploma.

At last, I ask what else they would like to comment on NUEE and mock exams. Mr. Wang says that his biggest wish is that the NUEE could be cancelled; but he says that he knows it is impossible and only his dream. He adds that the NUEE should be reformed and improved. Mr. Liang mentions homework. He says he does not mind doing homework, but he hopes that the homework is designed well for improving learning. Meanwhile, the other 4 students say nothing about the last question.

Part VI Analysis and Suggestions

1. In this research carried through questionnaire and interview, what impresses me most is that although students do not like exams, most of them think that exams are necessary and positive in enhancing learning; most of them do not oppose to the exam result and ranking being made public; they have been used to it and think it helps positive competition. This result makes me surprised in that most students say that they do not like exams; despite this, they accept them and see a positive side to them. Thus I propose a further question for a more detailed enquiry, which is the fourth question in the interview. The result is a further explanation; students say more about the positive effect of assessment in the learning progress. For example, Mr. Wang strongly opposes the cancellation of exams by saying that exams are very important. These show us the significance of assessment in schooling, as has being shown in Diagram 1. The way of assessing decides the actual impact of it. A good assessment system can exert its positive functions and an

inappropriate assessment system will hindered the progress of learning. As Dore says,

> *Schooling, and the certificates which attest to the schooling received, become what Fred Hirsch was later to call 'positional goods'—something whose value is not intrinsic but depends on how many other people have it. This process intensifies the examination- orientation of schooling, and while examination-orientation may beneficially intensify the effort to learn, it can also have 'backwash'—ill effects on the quality of learning as well as on subsequent attitudes towards the process of learning (1997: ix).*

This indicates the ill effects of examination-orientated schooling. At the same time, Dore says that,

> *In general education in language and literature, maths and science, examination clearly have their uses, with the exact form of the examination making quite a big difference to the kind of learning activity they encourage and hence to their usefulness. They provide informative feedback to teachers on how effective their teaching has been. For the pupil, the prospect of the sense of achievement at having done well in an examination can supplement the intrinsic pleasures of learning—satisfaction of curiosity, the sense of mastery, of growing and developing—by providing an incentive to*

stick at the tough slog—of puzzling out the difficult things, of continuous practicing and memorizing—that a lot of learning entails (1997: x).

Both from teachers' and students' points of view, this paragraph describes the usefulness of assessment in schooling and shows that assessment is an inevitable and important part of the learning and teaching process. From a sense related with society, Dore also points out that *examination can also serve to define what a society does count as a core citizen competence (1997, x).*

Besides these functions of educational assessment, Dore expresses his concerns about too much emphasis on assessment. He says that not all schooling is education. Much of it is mere qualification—earning— ritualistic, tedious, suffused with anxiety and boredom, destructive of curiosity and imagination; in short, anti-education (1997, ix).

Here I agree with his worries about education and schooling themselves since there has been a tendency of changing the students into machines for kinds of examinations rather than helping students for self-development (Su, 2004).

My research shows that this situation in this class is not bad. A majority of them take a positive attitude to their schooling. Though 58 percent of students think that the mock exams are a little too much, 94 percent students think mock exams are useful for them.

As a whole, my research shows that students do not feel disgusted with examinations. This suggests that the reform and endeavours the government has made in recent decades have had positive effects. Whereas, from another point of view, I cannot deny that these students just cannot help facing the serious situation but accepting it and getting used to it. The relatively positive results shown by this research cannot prove that Chinese education has been very good and helped to produce 'qualified citizens'. Chinese educational ideology is very different from western educational ideology. Chinese students have learned too much of obeying and passively receiving and accepting. Their imagination and creative capabilities have been unfortunately destroyed rather than been cultivated by schooling. In 1976, some one in the Chinese Education Department went to visit American schools. He found that the students there enjoyed much more freedom than Chinese students. They did not stick to one seat as in a Chinese class room. They could eat and drink and run around the classroom freely. When he came back, he wrote a report on it. He concluded his report by commenting that he felt so worried about the American education system and he thought America was in danger if they did not make changes. At the same time, some one in America also came to China for a visit to schools. He felt amazed that a Chinese class was so quiet and students were so obedient, they just sat straightly on their own chairs with arms behind their back. They held up their right hands when teachers asked questions and only the one who was nominated by the teacher could stand up to answer questions. He thought that this was very different from an American class. About three decades later, America is still prosperous and its education enjoys a high reputation around the world (Feng, 2004: A6). The Chinese education system has been reformed and improved many times and great improvement has been achieved. Whereas, students still have too much burden and they are still too much obedient (Su, 2004). A spirit of independence and innovation has still not been adequately exploited by our schooling. This should be noticed from the very beginning of education, which is primary school, or even from kindergarten.

2. Another point I would like to highlight here is the correlation between a diploma and students' actual capabilities which has been implied in the research. This point, I think, is closely related with the previous one. My ideal is that the diploma can accurately and fully reflect the holder's actual capability. The key point is the assessment criteria for the diploma. I do not believe that the 'diploma disease', so called by Dore, is a disease of the diploma itself; it is a disease of education as a whole. A diploma should be a good thing. It helps selection and differentiation. As Little says, the 'Diploma Disease' indicates that if the pursuit of certificates is

the socially legitimate way to improve one's life-chances in a society where resources are scarce and income and status differences great, then it is highly rational for individuals and their families to engage in their pursuit (Little, 1997: 7). The questionnaire feedback shows that 50 percent of students want to take the NUEE the next year in case of failing getting into university this year. For the other 50 percent students, the majority of them will take further study instead of entering university rather than looking for a job directly; because the diploma decides the category of jobs and the income to some degree. Dore has questioned whether it is rational for societies to allocate life chances based on educational certificates, whereas I do not think that it is not rational to depend on educational certificates for opportunity allocation. It is also one of the means of social management. What really matters, I think, is to improve the education system and assessment system itself. This situation demands a high-standard education system which can produce qualified citizens who hold the diploma. By saying this, I mean that a certain diploma can truly reflect the holder's actual comprehensive capabilities. This is, I think, one of the aims of the advocates of 'Quality Education'.

In past decades, there existed a phenomenon which is like what has been described by Dore,

In Britain, in 1900 you got a job in a newspaper

office by convincing the editor that you were as 'bright as a button'. By the middle of the century, there was no point in applying unless you had a 'good School certificate' (what later became O levels) to prove it (Dore, 1997: 25).

It is the same situation in China now. A position which can be successfully fulfilled by a graduate from 3-year college is usually competed for by hundreds of candidates who have Master's or even higher degree. This is one of the social reasons why the students are so eager to go to study at university and go on study for a post-graduate degree.

The questionnaire feedback shows that almost all the students in the target class want to go to university and all of them will take part in NUEE. Although they still have a choice such as vocational and technical colleges, they will only choose these colleges not so willingly in the case that they cannot enter university. As a result, a new problem arises in recent years. Little has said in 1997 that many of the old certainties about a good education leading to a good and secure job for life are breaking down (1997: 18). And she questions: in this changing context, what will become of the role of assessment in occupational allocation in global, national and local employment markets—and in guiding learning in the classroom (1997: 18).

The growth of upper levels of the school system goes so

far that the supply of capable low-qualification-level people dries up—as it did in Japan in the 1960s when employers found they simply couldn't get enough 15-year-olds to fill their blue-collar jobs because everybody was going on to high school (Dore, 1997: 192).

The recruitment practices of large firms may have shifted slightly from the cognitive dimensions signaled by academic records, towards greater emphasis on personality factors such as energy, initiative, self-assertiveness, or capacity for team-work (Dore, 1997: 195).

This is the very same condition now in China. It is reported that at the beginning of this year, a conference held for recruitment between one provincial vocational college and hundreds of companies showed that there has been an eager demand for senior blue-collar (technical worker), but the vocational college graduates obviously are fewer than the demand. Some big companies even raise the conditions on the spot for attracting graduates. Nevertheless, there are still quite a few companies leaving with no application from graduates (Jiang, 2004).

This slightly changed situation means good news beyond the severe competition for university entrance. This indicates that the situation has been changed from a somewhat irrational worship for educational certificates to a calmer selection. Moreover, this offers a direction for the primary and secondary schools education orientation.

It has been pointed by students that they want to learn the skills of getting along with others and society, they want to learn something more practical, more related with actual life beyond the knowledge only from books.

All these imply that the contemporary complex society is calling for a corresponding complexity in its education.

3. The third point I would like to highlight is the correlation between assessment and learning. It cannot be denied that assessment is an important part of the learning and teaching process. By offering feedback for students and teachers, and even to relevant governmental department, assessment can play a vital role and help enhancing learning. But since assessment has some functions beyond learning itself, it sometimes conflicts with learning. This point has been indicated as,

i. The current assessment system over emphasises the selection function; meanwhile, it ignores the function of enhancing students' learning improvement to some degree.

ii. The assessment criteria are a little monotonous, emphasizing the once-for-all academic results rather than evaluating the student's learning process.

iii. The methods of assessment are a little monotonous, attaching more importance to the written form, ignoring other assessment forms, emphasizing more about quantity rather than quality.

iv. The students are basically in a passive position in learning. There is a lack of protection for students' dignity and confidence. At the same time, students' capabilities of creativity are restrained rather than being developed. (Research Group of Curriculum Reform, 2003: 7)

These points summarize almost all the problems of school assessment in China. They are also supported by the questionnaire and interview feedback to some degree. Students still think that assessment is necessary and important and they agree that assessment really helps improve learning. What matters is the form of assessment, focus of assessment and method of assessment.

4. The last point in this part I would like to make is some suggestions for Chinese schooling derived from the analysis of the research feedback.

The first thing is about citizenship education. In feedback to the eighth question of the first part of the questionnaire, many students think that social morality and a sense for society should be appropriately assessed and taken into the consideration for university entrance. Other feedback from the questions shows that students emphasise the abilities of doing team-work and getting on well with others. This provokes me to ask whether they have taken citizenship education. I describe to them what citizenship education is, and all of them agree that it is necessary to take citizenship education.

Here I would like to refer to something about the importance, necessity and proposed content of citizenship education, linking it with the changing world situation and the tendency of globalization.

Globalization tends to change the world into a 'global village' both in space and time and the borders among states seem to recede. It is not possible that people in the world would be unified to have the same characteristics, due to the differences in history, tradition, custom, culture, etc. So relations among states should be interdependent and cooperative rather than those of assimilation. In this rapidly developing and changing world, to set one's standpoint and retain the characteristics of a certain state becomes more significant than ever before.

In Shandong Province, citizenship education as an independent subject has not been taken into the curriculum. Similar issues are usually dealt with in subjects such as history, geography and ideology education as students have said. Nowadays almost all the states are aware of the fact that education is the most potent means of development of the essentials of nationality (Green, 1997). Closely related with the sense of nationality, citizenship education is thus called upon to fulfil this task. As Cappella says, in this changing world, making the power of the vague sovereign state explicit is by and large a task of democratic educational institutions (2000: 232). Thus, it is a reasonable argument that the introduction of citizenship education as an independent subject is needed more than ever to provide a sense of purpose, solidarity, and guidance in a fragmented and a rapidly changing world (Pratte, 1988 quoted by Ichilov 1998: 271).

Politics is a basic dimension of citizenship. Issues of political significance arise frequently in subjects such as history, geography and religious education. This serves to remind us, if we needed reminding, that the curriculum is not a neutral thing, somehow extricated from its social and political context (Pearce & Hallgarten, 2000: 14).

Thus citizenship education should basically serve the interests of the nation (This statement applies, in particular, to the Chinese cultural context.). Simultaneously, in this changing world, the contents and patterns of citizenship education will, no doubt, have to be readjusted, in order to adequately prepare the younger generation to assume their role as citizens (Ichilov, 1998: 11). Here I would like to suggest that citizenship education should include the introduction of the changing situation of the world and the specific role of the individual country in the context of globalization.

Citizenship is a multidimensional conception. It is also an

indefinite and somehow disputed conception. Basically, citizenship conveys a sense of national identity combined with relevant rights and obligations, within which the development of the individual, relationships between individuals and relationships between people and the government are dealt with. Another major division would be: patriotism, nationalism, culture and politics.

In my opinion, citizenship education should mainly focus on these aspects. Moreover, a global consciousness should be promoted in this interdependent world. Here I fully agree with those Global educators on the precepts of 'Think globally, and act locally' in which that the global citizen would be skilled in the arts of peace-making; would have intercultural understanding; would be environmentally aware; would recognize human rights issues, and act on them; and would be able to imagine, and work for, alternative futures (Lister, 1998: 260). Although this still remains disputable within the relevant field, this proposal suggests a sound solution for citizenship education in this changing world. In the following paragraphs, a proposal of what should be included in the citizenship education syllabus would be discussed regarding to the multidimensional concept of citizenship and the changing situation.

The concept of citizenship contains a sense of the knowledge, skills, values and dispositions that, ideally, citizens should possess (Cogan, 1998: 2). As citizenship is a multidimensional concept, it would be confusing if there is not one unified conceptual framework for the concept. I would like herewith to adopt the five attributes of citizenship put forward by Cogan to be the main structure and mixed together with the other dimensions mentioned in the previous section. The five attributes are: a sense of identity; the enjoyment of certain rights; the fulfillment of corresponding obligations; participation; and an acceptance of basic societal values (Cogan, 2000: 2). Additionally, I would like to suggest a sixth attribute, Which is awareness of the globalised situation and the nation's orientation related to this changing world.

Another course suggested here is psychological education. Almost all the students being interviewed express their feelings of great pressure. They think that besides physical health, psychological health is of importance for them. I suggest that a course of psychological education, starting in primary school which directs students' life and study will do them good.

Additionally, Miss Jin says that she wants to take a course about individual financial management. I think this is an innovative point. Students spend a lot of their time at school. Beyond those knowledge that are now taught, the school is expected to educate students in more aspects to help them grow up to be qualified citizen. Primary school students in Belgium are taught about managing their pocket money, learning to be economical, buying cheaper stuff by waiting for the time of price reduction, etc (Feng, 2004: A6). In China, we have no such course like this. Additionally, courses about finance and economics could be considered into foundation education curriculum.

Another thing I would like to highlight is that the music course is only offered in Grade one of senior middle school, but some students who like music want to study much more than what is taught now. They want some more professional knowledge on it.

The questionnaire feedback and interview show that lots of students want the courses they are learning to be more practical, more related with real life. This reflects that the current courses are not practical enough and need to be improved. This is not only a call from students, but also a call from society, the employers. Dore comments on vocational courses that,

> *The form of the examination and the quality of the teaching on vocational courses, can cause students to forget about real life uses of the knowledge they are acquiring and concentrate exclusively on swotting for examination (1997: 28).*

This sentence explains the harms of an examination-oriented learning which puts too much emphasis on examinations rather than students' quality improvement. By saying this, I do not mean that Chinese education is not good, but it is a fact that Chinese education is still an examination-oriented one. Since there is slim possibility of canceling examinations at school, an improvement of examinations is necessary. Correspondingly, the curriculum should be reformed to go together with it. As has been suggested,

> *The school assessment should not only focus on students' academic marks, but also on cultivating and developing students' all-round potential capabilities, realizing students' needs in the development and helping students to know themselves well and build up a sense of confidence. We should emphasise the educational function of assessment to enhance students' development (Research Group of Curriculum Reform, 2003: 7).*

In addition, the design of curriculum should pay attention to cultivating students' creativity and a sense of independence; research on this shows that Chinese schools have not done a good job on it (Su, 2004). Another thing a lot of students show interest in is 'sociality'. This is expressed by the questionnaire and discussed further in interview. Mr. Gao says that every one is living together with others in the society. The way of dealing with the relationship with others and the whole society are important. He would like to take a course in such aspects.

In a word, a lot of valuable courses could be suggested here. To be able to catch up with the necessity of international exchange and international competition, the requirements for schooling, especially for foreign languages and world knowledge are increased to a new height. At the same time, national traditional cultural education and patriotism education should be strengthened. On the other side, a new series of subjects and knowledge should be included into the taught content of general education (In China, general education refers to those general schools distinguished from vocational education and technical education), such as population education, environmental education, economic education, technical education and vocational education, etc. (Jiang, 2001: 15).

It is impossible for students to take all of these subjects. Regarding this, I appreciate the system of A-level in the United Kingdom. A-level is the last two-year study before university. The students usually choose about three subjects among the available subjects. The chosen subjects are related with students' proposed major they will choose at university (Jiang, 2001: 91).

This system has its advantages as:

➢ The scope of choice is relatively wide.

➢ Students are free to choose the subjects they are willing to learn. This avoids the case that students are forced to learn what they have no interest in at all.

➢ The subjects they choose are preparatory courses for their future university study.

➢ Three subjects are not too much for students and it helps students to concentrate on their study.

By the analysis above, I suggest that Chinese schools consider a system of selective courses with one or two core compulsory courses to help students develop from their own interests and lessen students' burden at the same time. Furthermore, a positive curriculum setup would effectively help to enhance the 'Quality Education'.

Part VII Justification of the Validity and Reliability

When I am designing this research, the principles that guide the strategy I adopt are the issues of reliability and validity. Whatever procedure for collecting data is selected, it should always be examined critically to assess to what extent it is likely to be reliable and valid (Bell 1991:50).

Bell indicates that,

> *Reliability is the extent to which a test or procedure produces similar results under constant conditions on all occasions.*

Meanwhile,

> *validity tells us whether an item measures or describes what it is supposed to measure or describe. (Bell, 1991:51)*

What I am trying to achieve in this research design is to plan an appropriate and practical set of instruments which could enable me to get a most reliable and valid answer toward my research questions. Due to the limitation of the time, there are inevitable defects in this research. I would herewith point out two of them. One is about the degree of generalization. Since it is a small case study focused on a particular class of just 50 students, it is not justifiable to assert that my research result is representative of all the final year students in senior middle school in China. Another one is the absence in the research of close observation of students in the class, which would, I feel, have provided valuable data to increase the validity of those data obtained by less direct methods.

Trying to keep close with the research questions and obtain both reliability and validity, I elaborately plotted my design which will help connect the data collected with research questions.

Bell says that the aim of a research design is to obtain as representative a range of responses as possible to enable the researcher to fulfil the objectives of your study and to provide answers to key questions (Bell, 1991:52). Regarding the method employed, he proceeds to say,

Research instruments are selected and devised to enable you to obtain these answers. The instrument is merely the tool to enable you to gather data, and it is important to select the best tool for the job (Bell, 1999:52).

There are various instruments provided and suggested by research experts. It is not easy to assert which one is the best for a research. Since each research has its own style, characteristics and special purpose, the best tool for it should be the most appropriate one and the one which is possible to be handled at length according to the researchers' certain environment and conditions.

For answering the research questions, I employ interview as the main research tool and questionnaire as supplement and a pilot study for the interview.

As commonly happen, my research design is constrained by practical considerations and some compromises with the ideal are necessary. After careful evaluation, despite some weaknesses that I have indicated, I am confident that it is practical and efficient enough to achieve a minimum goal in maintaining the reliability and validity for my research task.

Part VIII Conclusions

Dore says that education is supposed to civilize people and improve the quality of life (1997: 26). I agree with his point and I think the objective of education is to 'produce' qualified citizens for a certain society. By 'qualified citizens', I mean citizens who have certain skills and capabilities of surviving and developing themselves and benefiting others and society at the same time. This means a serious task for education. Assessment is an important part of education. In China, National University Entrance Examination has been a significant examination for years. Through this research, conducted with a senior middle school graduate class, from a perspective of the Chinese NUEE and its impact, I am trying to highlight some of the problems now existing in Chinese schooling. Through an analysis of the relation between assessment and learning improvement, of the backwash effect of examination on the school teaching and learning process, I propose suggestions for the current educational focus in China, which is: curriculum reform for foundation education.

Besides, I still have two points to make about this

research.

One is that the target class is a class from one of the best schools in Shandong. This means that besides the small size of the class, this class can not present the whole situation in Chinese schools. Thus this leads to a problem I have noticed in the analysis of the questionnaire feedback. A majority of the students support their academic results being made public. They think this helps positive competition. Only 10 students think that they feel embarrassed about it. In the interview, almost all of the interviewees agree with the publication of their academic results; only Mr. Liang suggests sending the academic results to individual students, but he does not oppose the publication. This is, I think, because almost all the students in this class do fairly well in learning and examinations and hence they seldom feel ashamed of their academic results. This research result is against the advice in the fifth item of the sixth section of *Compendium for Curriculum Reform of Foundation Education (Draft),* which declares that the students' examination results should not be made public and there should be no rank list according to the results (Research Group of Curriculum Reform, 2003: 17). For this, I think that there is a danger that some students of the more successful students, such as those in this study, will lose some motivation if this item is carried out. What is better is to change it slowly according to different cases by reforming the assessment system to the core, especially the criteria for university entry; trying to evaluate students from a much broader scope beyond academic performance and trying to turn an achievement examination into an aptitude examination.

The NUEE should be reformed to match with the reform of the foundation education curriculum. Under the guideline of selecting personnel for university, helping implementing 'Quality Education' in middle schools, enlarging the administration rights of individual universities, the NUEE should strengthen its assessment of students' capabilities and quality; reform the content of assessment; offering multiple-chances a year for the selection modules (in China, we only have NUEE once a year), an open labour market and comprehensive evaluation (Research Group of Curriculum Reform, 2003: 17).

The comprehensive promotion of 'quality education' is an important part of the education system reform. 'Quality education' is not only related to the education structure, examination system and evaluation criteria, but also in connection with the education methods and concrete discipline. The proposition of 'quality education' is a deep touch to many problems existing in the exam-oriented education. The implementation of 'quality education' is a complex systematic project, which is closely associated with the overall situation and of great significance.

As a matter of fact, 'quality education' is a comprehensive and holographic conception. It's attributes are supposed to be reflected in all aspects of education. The purpose of 'quality education' is to convert all the knowledge building up in a gradual learning process into the students' intrinsic quality; then duly transform this quality to knowledge innovation ability and enhance the spirit of courage to explore the undiscovered fields.

Finally, I would like to refer to Dore here as the end of this report, with its implicit warning of the harm that can be done to an education system if a purely instrumental view of the role of assessment is allowed to dominate and define the basic purposes of education:

> *I resort to a rather simple typology of learning motives: learning for its own sake, learning to do a job, and learning to get a job. The first, and what I personally consider one of mankind's noblest activities, is self-explanatory. The crucial distinction is between the other two: learning to do a job, and learning to get a job. The first is good and necessary vocational education undertaken by people who have a reasonably clear notion of how they are going to earn their living, and want to learn how to do what they are going to do well. The second is learning simply to 'fulfil requirements'*

without either an intrinsic interest in what is learned or any conviction that it is necessary or even helpful knowledge for any subsequent job, learning undertaken solely with the intention of learning enough to pass the examination and get the qualification necessary for a job (Dore, 1997: 27).

Chapter Three

An Analysis of Speaking and Writing Skills Improvement during the Process of Second Language Acquisition

Language plays a crucial role in the development of human society. It is the main means of communication between individuals, groups and countries. Nowadays in China, more and more people are learning English as a second language. What is the effective method of learning a foreign language becomes their chief concern. Basically speaking, four modules are involved in the process of second language acquisition. They are listening, reading, writing and speaking. In English language teaching and learning, mastering these four modules means a lot. Speaking and writing skills, as the productive modules, are usually more difficult for learners. In this chapter, from the origin and functions of language, the correlation and disparities between speaking and writing skills are analyzed and possible ways of improving these two skills in second language acquisition are explored and suggested.

Part I Introduction

Kachru and Nelson suggest that English has developed from the native language of a relatively small island nation to the most widely taught, read, and spoken language that the world has ever known (2001: 9 cited in Kuo, 2006: 213). China, one of the leading emerging economies with the world's largest population, perhaps enjoys the largest population of ESL learners. With the proceeding and advancing of globalization, English learning and teaching attracts more and more attention in China. Meanwhile, improving English proficiency becomes a significant topic.

As for English proficiency, there are generally four basic skills involved in the language learning process. They are listening, reading, writing and speaking. Listening and reading are the processes of receiving, whereas, writing and speaking are processes of production, or put it another way, output.

In the case of first language acquisition, from traditional Chinese idea, the first thing to do should be listening, and then speaking and reading, writing usually comes the last. From my point of view, these four skills cannot be divided so clearly and they are interweaved with each other in the process of language acquisition. But the rough sequence is like this. Perhaps it is because of the different degrees of difficulty of these four skills. Generally speaking, receiving is much easier than producing and verbal process is easier than written things. However, in the case of second language learning, this sequence does not always work the same way.

In China, we usually start to learn a foreign language at the age of around 6 years old. This foreign language is often the English language. The general sequence of the four skills learning is: reading, listening, writing and speaking. This shows that writing and speaking, the productive skills, are comparably difficult for English language learners. Whereas, in the practical learning process, these four skills work together and help each other to improve. For example, when you are listening to the target language, this also helps to develop speaking skills. Furthermore, reading does the same to writing skills.

In this chapter, I will try to analyze the correlation and disparities between spoken language and written language to see how to apply them better in English language learning and teaching in China.

Part II The Characteristics and Importance of English Speaking and Writing skills

When discussing the origins of language, Yule mentions two functions of language:

> *"...All this noise-making and gesturing, seems to be characteristic of only one of the major functions of language use, which we may describe as the interactional function. It has to do with how humans use language to interact with each other, socially or emotionally; how they indicate friendliness, co-operate or hostility, or annoyance, pain, or pleasure.*
>
> *But there is another major function of language, the transactional function, whereby humans use their linguistic abilities to communicate knowledge, skills and information..." (1996: 6).*

In this paragraph, Yule points out the interactional function and transactional function of language. These two functions share a common point: communication between human beings.

Languages originated from the need for communication between and among people. From this 'need', spoken language appeared and developed, and then the written language, which catered for the need of recording and preserving things. To put it simply, the purpose and the function of language is to know about other people and let others know about you. Listening and reading are processes for the former and speaking and writing accomplish the task of the latter. To learn a foreign language, it is necessary to master all of these four skills. It is incorrect to suppose that you can listen to others and read materials in the target language but cannot speak and write in it at all. Language is a tool of communication of human society. This kind of communication is a bi-directional process which includes both receiving information as well as giving out information. This giving-out includes speaking and writing. In a long period, writing capability is considered to be the symbol of the well-educated. In some sense, we can say that writing skills are more advanced than speaking skills. In the case of first language acquisition, speaking is learned unconsciously in daily life and writing is learned consciously, usually in schools. But in the second language learning situation, speaking is of no easier than writing. There are various reasons for the characteristics and differences of these two skills. Here I would like to state two of them.

The first one is the learning environment. For writing, it is usually not so difficult to obtain and refer to written materials. But speaking is a skill which demands more practice in daily life. In China, English language is not used widely. Except for some loanwords from English, we seldom use English in our daily lives. For an English language learner, the English class is almost the only language environment for him/her to learn and practice English. But the classroom is only an artificial language environment. Chinese English language learners lack favourable conditions for language acquisition.

Another difficulty for learning English speaking skills regards grammar.

> *"...There is, to begin with, no influential description of spoken English which has, say, the status of grammars of written English. Spoken English appears very variable, and is very different from one dialect area to another. Even between speakers who mostly speak 'standard English' there is different emphasis in their selection from forms in standard English. ..." (Brown, 1983: 3).*

Grammar offers a set of rules for language, according to which we can comprehend and produce correct language alternatives. For English writing, there are plenty of rules for us to abide by. Whereas, we could hardly find specialized grammar for speaking skills. Sometimes, Chinese English language learners speak according to the rules of writing. But speaking is not just uttering the exact written language. Another point is that native speech varies from area to area, from culture to culture, between different age groups, different levels of education, from different social classes etc. What and How should we teach spoken English? It is an issue which has been discussed by scholars for years and is still subject to debate, since spoken language is both inconstant and changeable.

Part III Correlation and Disparities between Spoken Language and Written Language

In one sense, we can say that written language is the written form of what people speak. The difference between them is that one is oral and one is written. But the case is not so simple. These two forms of language perform different functions in human society and the different functions determine their fundamental differences.

Although both of them are processes of production, written language is not just spoken language written down and spoken language is not the written language read aloud. It is usual practice that people use different words and sentence structures to express the same thing in writing and speaking. Take the read-aloud case for example:

> *"Of course if you have actually tried to 'speak like a book' yourself, you may agree that it can be hard work. It is hard work reading aloud from a book. This may be because it is not something we are used to; or because*

the sentences can be awkward to read aloud—too long, too complex, or too technical. It can be tricky to get the correct intonation, and you may find you often have to re-read bits to make them sound right. Reading aloud tends to require considerable attention. " (Bygate, 1991: 10).

When I am in junior middle school, in the English class, it is common practice to read some certain text aloud. This is a case of speaking written language. From some Chinese English teachers' point of view, reading the text aloud can help students to get a more profound impression about it and practice their pronunciation and intonation. But the language which is spoken out is far away from everyday spoken language.

The following statements summarize some of the differences between these two forms of language skills:

a) Written language tends to use longer and more complex sentences and the sentence of spoken language is shorter and easier to understand.

b) Written language usually allows for a second thought but spoken language is often produced on the spur of the moment.

c) Written language usually lasts longer and spoken language is comparably transient, except in the case of audio recordings.

d) Written language usually tends to transmit information. However, spoken language tends to express more emotions and personal feelings, perform more functions in smoothing interpersonal relations.

These points are only a small part of their differences.

Since written language and spoken language are different in so many ways, we recognize that we should follow different procedures for dealing with them in English language learning and teaching.

Part IV How to Deal with Spoken Language in English Language Learning and Teaching

When I was a middle school student, teachers put more attention on reading and writing and provide less practice with listening and speaking. Consequently, listening and speaking skills are always my weakness in English. It is a wide-spread problem for English language learners of my age in China. To sum up the reasons:

a) The national syllabus for English language teaching places more emphasis on reading and writing than on listening and speaking.

b) The teaching conditions and teachers' proficiency are limited with regard to listening and speaking skills.

c) Listening and speaking skills are not basic requirements for assessment.

d) The social environment does not demand much for English listening and speaking skills.

However, things have changed considerably in

recent years. With reference to the above,

a) The national syllabus has changed gradually to emphasize all of the four skills of English language learning, and the teaching materials have been greatly improved for this purpose.

b) The teaching conditions have been improved and some of Chinese schools now have specialized language laboratories. And some of the schools have engaged more native English language speakers to teach spoken English.

c) As regards assessment procedures, listening and speaking are given equal emphasis as reading and writing skills and a relatively complete English language assessment system has been implemented. As assessment has a backwash for learning and teaching. That is, what is assessed determines what is taught and learned. Teachers and students must work hard to improve listening and speaking skills to satisfy the assessment.

d) In recent years, the English language has been used much more widely in China. For example, more and more foreign companies whose official language is English have entered Chinese market. If a student wants to work for the foreign companies, a good English speaking proficiency would provide him/her a better opportunity.

In addition, here I would like to put forward two international tests for English language to illustrate this change. About two decades ago, TOEFL was very popular in China and it occupied a dominant status for English language test. When IELTS came up, it gradually becomes more and more popular as a significant test indicating learner's English language level. The big difference between these two forms of test is that IELTS put more emphasis on assessing learner's practical capability in using the spoken language. If the learner wants to get a satisfactory result in IELTS test, he/she must work hard to obtain a good English spoken skill.

All these changes have had fundamental effects on English language learning and teaching in China. Teachers and learners pay much more attention to practical usages of English language, especially the learning of spoken language. How to learn and how to teach spoken language are attracting more and more attention.

At the very mention of spoken language, what comes first to my mind is that related to pronunciation and intonation. Undoubtedly, they are two of the basic elements for speaking a language. For a beginner, it is not surprising that he/she spends a considerable time on repeating some certain vowels or consonants and on trying to distinguish between similar sounds. The exactness of pronunciation is really of great importance. I have heard a story from my friend. When he was in London waiting for the coach to Bath, he wanted to confirm if that bus stop was the very stop for his coach and asked a man standing beside. Unfortunately, great confusion occurred between them concentrating on the words 'Bath' and 'bus'. That man kept saying, 'yes, this is the bus stop' in reply to his enquiry. This is a problem of the similar pronunciation of 'th' and 's'. This story shows us how important the right pronunciation is. It really affects our daily lives greatly.

In China, spoken English is usually taught and learnt in these ways: model dialogues, pattern practice, oral drill tables, look-and-say exercises, oral composition, etc. Sometimes we have group discussion and, very occasionally, we hold debates on particular issues for the purpose of practicing spoken English.

However, this is far away from enough. Spoken language is such complex a system and the learners must learn much more things besides these.

How is spoken language produced? Is it to read the written language aloud together with some oral expressions? Or is it another completely different language system? These are difficult questions to answer. Here I would like to quote from Bygate when he is discussing how to learn spoken language. After citing some traditional methods for learning spoken language, he says,

"Ten years later, during which time this approach to teaching oral skills had been widely adopted, David Wilkins pointed out there were some learning problems that exercises like these did not solve. An important one is that of ensuring a satisfactory transition from supervised learning in the classroom to real-life use of the skill. This transition is often called the 'transfer of skills'. " (1991: 6).

Here he mentions the 'transfer of skills' from classroom learning to real-life. This is really a widespread problem in China, where the English language learning environment is not sufficient enough. But we have tried to make more opportunities for students keep in frequent touch with English. It is very helpful to bring up something that attracts students' interests. The English corner is a very good example. English corner is a certain place for people to gather together with each other to talk in English language. In Jinan, the city where I live, we have an English corner in the central city park. Most of them are students and teachers and also some native speakers. They talk on various issues and exchange their ideas in English. English corner constitutes a kind of microcosmic English language environment.

As for the method of learning and teaching spoken English, the Audiolingual method is worth mentioning here,

"Audiolingual method, a very different approach, emphasizing the spoken language, became popular in the

1950s. This involved a systematic presentation of the structures of the L2, moving from the simple to the more complex, often in the form of drills which the students had to repeat. This approach, called the Audiolingual method, was strongly influenced by the belief that the fluent use of a language was essentially a set of 'habits' which could be developed with a lot of practice" (Yule, 1996: 193).

The audiolingual method emphasizes the learning of spoken language. It is disputable due to its own disadvantages. But I appreciate the idea of 'habits' mentioned here. Practice makes perfect. When the learner practices the spoken language more and more, a set of habits can be formed inside him/her, which would make him/her to produce spoken language in L2 from consciously to somewhat unconsciously and speak the L2 more naturally.

Besides the factors mentioned above, there is a major problem still exists for English language learners in speaking skills. As the civilization and society are advancing, the function of maintaining interpersonal relationship in spoken language is becoming more and more prominent.

"...in a reciprocal exchange, a speaker will often have to adjust his or her vocabulary and message to take the listener into account. The speaker also has to participate actively in the interlocutor's message—asking

questions, reacting and so on. This is something which requires an ability to be flexible in communication, and a learner may need to be prepared for it. " (Bygate, 1991: 8).

This means that even if you can pronounce the right sentence with proper intonation, it is still not enough. Perhaps there are quite a few words and sentence structures to express the same meaning. Which one should be employed for the best purpose of communication and smoothing the relationship at the same time? In order to communicate successfully, the learner must have mastered most of the language skills and have a considerable understanding of the certain culture where the L2 is spoken and then have the ability to handle variational situations freely. This is really a high demand for an L2 learning.

Another difficulty arises when we consider that English language varies from country to country and even from area to area. It is not so easy to say what is standard English. British English? American English? Canadian English? Australian English? Singapore English? And still many other kinds of English. They are all English but they are different in many ways, from lexical choosing to intonation employment. To deal with these variations in English language, we introduced more and more authentic materials to our English language learning class for students to listen to and have a general grasp about it. And students are encouraged to listen to BBC as well as Voice of America and try to imitate British English or American English.

Spoken language is flexible and open to change. It is not easy to get a good mastery of the spoken language in the L2. But it is possible to establish a good basis in pronunciation and the grammar of the target language. When it is possible to apply it to real life, the learner will make it soon. I am an example of this. My spoken English is not very good in China. When I first came to England, I really found listening and speaking difficult. But after 3 months, I feel it much easier for me to communicate with others in various circumstances. The greatest difference from China is that I am in an English speaking environment here. From my own point of view, this circumstance is of vital importance for English language learners for speaking good English. That is the very reason why I came here to study and live for a year.

Part V Dealing with Written Language in English Language Learning and Teaching

Yule points out that:

> *"When we consider the development of writing, we should bear in mind that a very large number of the languages found in the world today are used only in the spoken form. They do not have a written form. For those languages which do have writing systems, the development of writing, as we know it, is a relatively recent phenomenon..." (1996: 9).*

Written language appeared much later than spoken language and initially it just wrote down what people spoke. But with the development of different special purposes of writing, written language developed its own style and own rules and became a highly-demanded skill of language. In a very long period, writing is always a symbol indicating person's educational level. In TOEFL and IELTS tests, the written module is usually considered to be the decisive module. Many universities or colleges' English proficiency entrance requirement is like this, IELTS overall band no less than … with writing module no less than …

In China, we always put attention on English writing. Unlike speaking skills, writing is much more constant and has relatively stable grammar to refer to. In this sense, learning to write in English is not so difficult as learning to speak in English. But learning to write proper English is a very hard work.

> *"An ability to speak well—fluently, persuasively, appropriately— is something that most of us would hope to achieve in our first language. It is also an objective for many learners of a foreign language, especially those who wish to do business internationally, or to study to travel in English speaking countries. An ability to write appropriately and effectively is, however, something which evades many of us, in our mother tongues or in any other languages we may wish to learn, and this in spite of the many years which are frequently devoted to the development of the skill. " (Tribble, 1997: 3).*

Even in the case of first language acquisition, people need to learn writing in their mother tongue on purpose, usually in schools. It is no wonder that we consider writing a difficult skill to learn in the case of second language learning.

For writing, the learner should first have a good mastery of English vocabulary which would make it possible for him to choose the most appropriate words for his/her writing. Besides this, he/she is expected to be good at various sentence structures and have a relatively full knowledge of English grammar. At last, he/she should lay out a logical outline for his/her writing as a whole.

Here I would still like to recommend authentic materials for students to read. By 'authentic materials' here, I mean the materials written by native English-speaking authors. Read more and practice more would help the learner to write much more like native speakers.

Writing is indeed a big issue in language learning. It is not easy trying to cover all its aspects in this chapter here. It is an advanced and important skill for a foreign language learner.

Part VI Conclusion

The function of language is to communicate with others to survive and to maintain certain interpersonal relationships. As two skills of language, speaking and writing have their own characteristics and they have fundamental differences in many respects. This requires different learning and teaching methods to deal with them respectively.

There are different examples regarding learning and teaching spoken language and written language. As an English teacher in China, how to apply both of them appropriately to the classroom is of vital importance. Language is a changeable system, especially the spoken language. It really seems impossible to work out a perfect plan of how to learn and teach spoken language and written language. What we can do is to do our best to improve the better methods and materials and map out different teaching plans for the various needs of English learners.

Chapter Four

An Analysis of Effective Writing Skills in Business English

Part I Introduction

In recent years, the international financial market turbulence has intensified, spreading from partial regions to almost the whole world, from developed countries to emerging economies, from the financial field to the real economy. All of these have posed severe challenges to countries all over the world.

Mr. Greenspan has described it as a financial crisis once in one hundred years; what's worse, there is still no obvious sign of reaching the bottom. What sort of consequences will it bring for the global real economy? What impact will it have to emerging markets? What changes will happen to the global financial system? These problems perplex inhabitants of the 'global village'.

Economic globalization could be listed as one of the most important condition for economic development of all countries. The globalization of financial markets, based on a stable international financial system, is the core of economic globalization. Since the collapse of the gold standard, the international financial system, as a global public product, is the outcome of human design. A serious problem is likely to appear with thirty years as a cycle. To address this issue, proper adjustment or restructuring are necessary. Financial globalization is the market mechanism of intertemporal allocation of global resources under uncertain conditions, the crisis of it means global economic crisis, and its collapse implies the breakup of economic integration. This is a profound enlightenment we have obtained from the past one hundred and fifty years in the process of world economy picture.

In the process of globalization deepening, one of the priorities is bringing up compound high-quality business talents who are acquainted with the international economic environment, international business norms and are proficient at intercultural business communication with a global vision.

With the deepening of the global financial crisis caused by the subprime mortgage crisis in the United States, the trend of protectionism has risen. This point has been reconfirmed by American presidential election in 2017. Free trade and market opening have been significantly affected and this has had a negative impact on the global economy. At the same time, international economic and trade patterns will change significantly

For the western developed countries, the challenge is to amend and adjust the original international financial order. As far as China is concerned, the crisis provides us with an historical opportunity to expand the national outlook, shifting from a passive recipient of vested interests to become a constructive partner within the world's political and economic pattern. The key to seizing this rare opportunity lies in whether we have a large pool of talents equipped with international business knowledge.

The Belt and Road， abbreviated as B&R, is put forward in 2013 by President Xi Jinping, referring to the strategic concept—building of the 'new Silk Road Economic Belt' and 'twenty-first Century Maritime Silk Road'.

'The Belt and Road' is more than a substantive or mechanism. In stead, this conception embraces great ideas and initiatives of cooperation and development, which relies on the established and effective platform for regional cooperation between China and relevant partner countries as well as the existing bilateral and multilateral mechanisms. The idea is to hold high the banner of peaceful development under the guideline of the historical symbol 'Silk Road' and actively develop economic partnership with countries along the road, in an endeavour to build a common-interest community involving political trust, economic integration and cultural inclusion.

In recent years, once popular English graduates are faced with the embarrassment of difficulty in seeking for desirable jobs. There still exists a big gap between the general English language and business English which covers knowledge both in international trade and the financial system. Business English, as an independent field of discipline, find its space for development at universities and colleges. University of International Business and Economics offers not only business English studies but also business English Ph. D. Shandong University of Finance and Economics also set up business English department to offer relevant courses. This has proved to be a wise decision, evidencing by the steadily increasing growth of freshperson.

Business English writing has a wide range of applications. Besides covering trade letters in the traditional sense, it also includes correspondence in daily work. In addition, cover letters, reports, and proposals are integral parts of business writing. From a practical point of view, the ability to communicate through business letters is one of the basic skills required for each practitioner to succeed in his or her career. Especially with the development and popularization of the Internet, the use of the Internet for information communication is becoming increasingly frequent and routine, which put forward more urgent requirements for business English writing ability. The ability to write effectively is regarded as a valuable business asset. This chapter is designed to analyze problems existing in business writing from several perspectives as shown below.

Part II Interchangable Use of Synonyms

In English reading materials, the phenomenon of synonym conversion is widely spread. This helps to make the wording of the article rich and vivid. In addition, it helps the readers to figure out some new words without dictionary to understand the text thoroughly.

According to Wikipedia, the free encyclopedia, a synonym is a word or phrase that means exactly or nearly the same as another word or phrase in the same language. Words that are synonyms are said to besynonymous, and the state of being a synonym is called synonymy. An example of synonyms is the words begin, start, commence, and initiate. Words can be synonymous when meant in certain senses, even if they are not synonymous in all of their senses. For example, if one talks about a long time or an extended time, long and extended are synonymous within that context. Synonyms with exact meaning share a seme or denotational sememe, whereas those with inexactly similar meanings share a broader denotational or connotational sememe and thus overlap within a semantic field. Some academics call the former type cognitive synonyms to distinguish them from the latter type, which they call near-synonyms.

Some lexicographers claim that no synonyms have exactly the same meaning (in all contexts or social levels of language), because etymology, orthography, phonic qualities, ambiguous meanings, usage, etc. make them unique. Different words that are similar in meaning usually differ for a reason: feline is more formal than cat; long and extended are only synonyms in one usage and not in others (for example, a long arm is not the same as an extended arm). Synonyms are also a source of euphemisms. Euphemistic expressions are used in business English more often than not. These add the importance of synonym using in effective business writing. On the other hand, one thing to be observed is that employing of more advanced synonyms calls for strict appropriateness. Otherwise, the effective writing could not be achieved. In this sense, English learners are supposed to not only have a good possession of synonyms, but also understand the exact meaning of each word and their usage in various contexts. This demands a depth of learning words on the basis of large quantity.

As has been mentioned above, these synonyms sharing the same meaning reflect diverse styles and colors. Some of them are neutral words, which are used in general occasions.

While other words are used in different styles, such as in written and academic cases. Generally speaking, these synonyms can be divided into general words and specific words. In particular, the specific vocabulary is generally more complex, and the meaning of the expression is more appropriate and suitable to concrete situations. These features of vocabulary are of great significance to the improvement of business English writing.

The level of writing is one of the important criteria to measure the author's language proficiency, this not only contains ideological content, the layout, sentence structure, etc. , but also the diversity of the usage of words.

In various English tests, 'lexical diversity' always plays a vital part in the scoring criteria for writing. TOEFL, IELTS, BEC and other international reputable English examinations tend to use the diversity of words as one of the criteria for writing tasks. Therefore, the diversity of words is an important criterion to measure the effectiveness of English writing. In order to meet this standard, English learners are supposed to pay attention to the conversion of synonyms in English writing. To achieve this purpose, it is necessary to accumulate more synonyms in everyday English study. Such being the case, I would like to recommend several suggestions to help reaching this goal.

First thing I would like to deal with is about methodology.

It is a good attempt to encourage students to identify synonyms in reading process. In English teaching, teacher should first explain the rules and methods of synonyms conversion in English language. In the course of intensive or extensive reading, teachers can instruct learners to find out the involved synonyms encountered in typical sentences and paragraphs, then encourage learners bear them in mind. This approach helps to strengthen learners' awareness of synonyms and to develop the habit of using synonyms in reading and writing and improve their writing ability and autonomous learning ability. For extensive reading, English business news from BBC or CNN furnish excellent genuine materials to study; do not forget to screen out some biased political tendencies.

The second point I would like to make is about the using of dictionary. In the process of everyday English learning, a majority of learners tend to use English-Chinese dictionary, usually network dictionary nowadays, to aid in the interpretation of new words. With the increase of vocabulary, learners should try to avoid using Chinese to translate or interpret unknown words. Language is the carrier and embodiment of ways of thinking. If we develop the habit of interpreting English in English, it will help us to think in English way and develop more idiomatic English in writing. In addition, the interpretation of English in English will help learners to enrich their vocabularies and expressions, so as to improve their writing capability effectively.

English learners should be encouraged to conduct extensive English reading after class. In the reading process, it is strongly recommended to summarise and accumulate a large amount of synonyms and their practical usage on purpose, which forms a solid foundation for the synonyms conversion in the writing process. Special attention should be paid to those frequently used words and expressions. Besides doing this, a large number of English writing exercises are required. At this stage, the application of synonyms conversion strategy is supposed to be observed. Doing this not only ensures the accurate syntactic structure, but also assists to achieve the vocabulary rich diversity, which involves properly switching between synonyms. The idea is to select the most appropriate specific word to express your idea or intention adequately, thus to produce effective English essays.

As has been elaborated above, it is better to use words with specific meanings instead of general words to make the language more vivid and accurate. Another strategy that could be adopted is to shift the part of speech of certain words to achieve the purpose of synonymous translation. This approach only changes the word order of the sentence, or shifts the focus of the sentence, without altering the original meaning. Therefore, it is necessary to pay attention to the accurate discrimination of different parts of speech sharing the same word root, which always remains a problem for quite a few English learners.

Sometimes, in the article, we will use the semantic word and the subordinate word alternatively: the upper words and the lower words. For instance, *animal* covers tiger, leopard, dog, lion, etc. It is also recommended to use the antonyms of words to replace them, namely, plus negative prefixes or negative words to form antonyms. This measure can also achieve synonymous substitution effect.

To conclude, English language is a rich and specific language rather than general one as somebody thought. Its vocabulary body embraces a great variety of meaningful, concrete and vivid words and expressions. The same meaning could be delivered in different words and expressions according to different contexts. This adds difficulties in words memorising undoubtedly. Whereas, it is one of the many reasons of why English language are attractive and appealing. When writing English, special attention should be paid to diversity of vocabulary option and the sentence structure selection. Consequently, English learners should pay attention to synonyms acquisition and accumulation as well as synonymous alteration in the writing process in an effort to enrich vocabulary and improve English writing performance eventually.

Part III Deployment of Euphemistic Strategy in Business English

With the rapid development of social economy, international trade exchanges become increasingly frequent than old days, in which business correspondence plays a significant role. Business correspondence constitutes a large part of international business negotiation. A prosperous firm deals with a plenty of business letters everyday. Here, the conception of 'letters' include emails or other message-delivering forms with the same function. Every business message is designed to achieve a specific business objective. Its success lies in what it says and to what extent it induces a favourable response from the addressee. An English business letter with proper courtesy, not only assists to set up a good enterprise image, but also helps to maintain sustainable business relationships. Courtesy principle falls into the established criteria of six Cs for effective business English writing. Unfortunately, not a few English learners find it hard to express themselves appropriately and consider it as a difficult mission. One of the reasons is that they haven't realised the vitality of courtesy strategies in writing or they are unable to deploy this strategy properly. This part aims at putting forward the methodology which will help to achieve tactful diction and friendly tone during business negotiation process. By doing this, the possibility of consummating a certain transaction will be significantly increased.

In the 1960s, Grice pointed out that both parties involved in a negotiation are supposed to comply with some primary rules, among which involving "cooperative principle" and "politeness principle" (Grice, 1975: 26), to ensure the favourable outcome of the related communication. From his perspective, both parties share the common goal: understanding each other and collaborating to reach an agreement. In this sense, they observe these principles for the sake of common interests. In the 1980s, English linguistician Leach made a further statement based on Grice's principles. He proposed the politeness principle that the writers and the receivers should maximize the expression of polite beliefs and minimize the expression of impolite beliefs from the aspects of rhetoric and pragmatics (Leech, 1983: 65).

Review of actual business correspondence demonstrates that special attention should be devoted to ensuring the courtesy of business communication. Courtesy means treating people with respect and friendly human concern. Effective writers visualise the reader before starting to write. As a saying goes, do not judge unless you've walked in his or her shoes for miles. Reader's desires, problems, circumstances, emotions and probable reactions to the request, all of these should be taken into consideration before initiating a business letter.

Creating a sense of courtesy in a letter usually includes three aspects: using you-viewpoint, taking a positive tone and being conversational (Hu, 2013: 2). These three steps help to build up a polite atmosphere of business communication and avoid potential misunderstanding, especially instructive in a disputable circumstance.

For this topic, I have to mention what is called as Chinglish. One of the prominent features of Chinglish is that it is fairly weak in expressing the author's idea clearly, which fails to achieve the effect of courtesy, sometimes even accomplish the very opposite. Especially in CET-4 and CET-6 bands examinations, this is a main cause of poor performance in writing task. To get rid of Chinglish, it is an effective way to observe and distinguish the differences between Chinese and English, subsequently avoid Chinese style in English business writing.

Due to the diverged ways of thinking, English and Chinese are very different in many aspects. Some of the following points may illustrate this point.

Compared with Chinese, English tends to express itself more statically; in other words, nouns are used more frequently in English language. This suggests that the conscious use of nouns will help in writing more effectively. For instance,

In order to get greater market share, we will have to bring out a new type of machines on the basis of the improvement of our current ones.

In Chinese, it means “为了赢取更多的市场份额，我们必须在改进现有产品的基础上，生产一款新的机器。” The word ‘improvement’ is a noun in English; its part of speech changes into verb as embodied in Chinese version, “改进”.

Using of nouns improve a sense of formality, which is greatly valued in business circumstance.

Another tactic is related with passive voice. Passive voice is one of the characteristics of English language. Although there are similar sentence structure existing in Chinese featured by “被” ，this is very different from English passive voice. Passive voice is one of the most effective means to realize courteous business English communication. It makes people feel more objective, thus weakening the contrariety and achieving the purpose of effective communication. Although some certain studies have shown that English learners tend to exert excessive use of passive voice because of teachers’ repeated emphasis, this should not be taken as a reason of discouraging the use of passive voice. In order to achieve good communication under business circumstance, the key lies in proper usage of passive voice. For example,

The matter was brought to the board of directors.

已把此事项提至董事会。

In this sentence, who brought the matter does not really matter. This kind of expression is effective in exerting the function of informing.

In the passive voice sentence, the subject is generally the object item. In addition, there is another feature in English language that is distinguished from Chinese—objective subject. The subject of Chinese is usually I, We, You, He, She, They, etc. But if these appear as subject in most of the English sentences, it will inevitably become the symbol of Chinglish. English is a subject-prominent language, which means subject in English language tend to be longer. In other words, many sentences have big heads. This difference is worth noticing in English language reading and writing. To achieve this effect, objective subject offers a good choice as well as the employment of the passive voice. The following example may furnish a sound evidence,

Edward's academic background, his teaching experience and his track record in the field of micro-enterprise development are testimony to his

dedication, energy and enthusiasm with which he tackles any project at hand. (Hu, 2013:221)

This sentence possesses a big head, a long subject in other words. The subject runs from the very beginning of the sentence to the word *development*. It constitutes exactly half of the whole sentence.

The passive voice and the objective subject strategies effectively avoid too many of 'I', 'We', 'You' and other subjective expression, thus escape the Chinese style in English writing. Felicitous deployment of objective subject is fairly important for effective euphemistic expression in business English writing.

The previous example also supplies an example for long and complex sentence in business English, another instance is shown as follows,

The artificially low prices caused by excess capacity and unfairly-traded imports suppress profits in the American steel industry.

The subject of this sentence is also very long, accounting for more than half of the sentence. Like the previous example, it is a typical case of objective subject. This sentence contains adverbs, adjectives, compound postpositive attribute and temporal adverbials, which fully project the complexity of English sentence structures. In writing, correct and appropriate use of long sentences is also one of the important ingredients of euphemistic expression. When writing complex sentences, sentence structure, order of constituents and their reciprocal relationships require careful attention in an effort to avoid vague statements.

Part IV Conclusion

In addition to the above parts of the discussion, correctness in writing could not be neglected in order to achieve an appropriate and euphemistic business communication, especially avoiding sentence fragment, run-on sentence and comma splice—these common stylistic problems.

Correct grammar, punctuation and spelling are basic requirements for effective business writing. Errors made in business letters and reports have a negative impact on the reputation of the company and the writer concerned. Such errors tend to distract the reader's attention from the information conveyed itself and thereby decrease the effectiveness. Besides, you should also watch for common types of errors: misplaced elements and dangling modifiers in business letters, because these could cause confusion to the addressee. To avoid misplaced elements, you should place words, phrases or clauses near the words they modify. Placing words, phrases or clauses in the wrong position is likely to perplex the reader. (Hu, 2013: 5)

This chapter analyzes some problems to be noted in business English writing according to the principles of effective communication and courtesy, and thereafter puts forward several specific countermeasures to avoid Chinglish through the careful analysis of the characteristics and difficult points of business English in an effort to realize a euphemistic and effective business communication.

One more thing worth noticing is that in recent years, business English words tend to be more neutral. Traditional *chairman* shifts into a *chairperson* as more and more ladies come into power in prominent positions. The same case also happens to these words: *salesman* to *salesperson*; *freshman* to *freshperson*; etc. This slight but significant change reflects the further advancement of female in the world, an embodiment of gender equality in language. The appearance of these sorts of words also represents an aspect of euphemistic business expression.

Chapter Five

Morphology Theory and Its Application in English Learning

Part I Introduction

As a field of language study, morphology attracts lots of attention both from linguistics field as well as from language learning and teaching domain. Morphology aims at analyzing how the words are composed of. Words are basic units of language. Fromkin said,

> *Knowing a language means knowing the words of that language.*
>
> *(Fromkin, 1998: 96)*

Obviously, this sentence tends to be a little over-stated about the importance of words since there still exist things like sentence structure etc. But it undoubtedly tells us what a significant role that words are playing in language. In language teaching and learning practice, words are usually the first thing for students to learn, and then extend to sentences and to the whole text.

Words in languages are always of a huge amount. Especially in the case of second language acquisition, the learner would find it a very hard work to remember the new words of the target language. Fortunately, morphology offers a solution to the seemingly boundless vocabulary sea and shows us certain rules of words composition, which makes it much easier to master a second language. In this chapter, as an English teacher in China, I'd like to elaborate some views on the analysis of morphology and on how it could be used in assisting the English language learning and teaching.

Part II What is Morphology?

The study of the internal structure of words, and of the rules by which words are formed, is called morphology (Fromkin, 1998: 69).

Here, after the definition of morphology, Fromkin gives an example regarding the word 'morphology' itself to illustrate it in details:

> *This word itself consists of two morphemes, morph+ology. The morphemic suffix—ology means "science of" or "branch of knowledge concerning." Thus, the meaning of morphology is "the science of word forms".*
>
> *(Fromkin, 1998: 69)*

As a part of grammar, morphology takes morphemes as its study object. The definition of a morpheme is,

> *'a minimum unit of meaning or grammatical function'.*
>
> *(Yule, 1996: 75)*

Whereas, Bloomfield defines a morpheme as

> *a linguistic form that bears no partial phonetic-*

semantic resemblance to any other form.

(Palmer 1983: 99)

Yule and Palmer describe morphemes from different points of view. To look at both of them, we could get a more full conception of what a morpheme is.

Part III How Does the Morphemes Work in Language?

As part of grammar, morphology offers a set of rules in word formation and this makes it possible to make predictions of the meaning of the words. When having mastered a certain amount vocabulary of a target language and know something about the rules of morphology, it is likely to guess the meaning of a new word, especially according to the context. Although it is not always so exact, it really helps a lot in language learning.

For example, suppose the word 'writer' is new to the learner. But from his background knowledge about English language, he knows the meaning of the verb 'write'. He also knows— -er is a derivational morpheme which changes a verb into noun and indicates the person who carries out the action of the verb. From these, it is possible for him to guess that the meaning of the word 'writer' is the person who writes. Of course, it is not always exact to guess the meaning of a word. For the exact and complete definition, it is better to consult the dictionary. But this kind of guess really helps in target language reading comprehension. Here is another example,

> *...let's look at some sample data, adapted from examples originally presented in Gleason (1955), and try to work out which morphological features can be identified. The first is from Kanuri, a language spoken in Nigeria.*
>
> *Kanuri*

('excellent')	*karate*	*-n mkarite*	*('excellence')*
('big')	*kura*	*-n mkara*	*('bigness')*
('small')	*gana*	*-n mgana*	*('smallness')*
('bad')	*dibi*	*-n mdibi*	*('badness')*

> *From this set, we can propose that the prefix n m- is a derivational morpheme which can be used to derive nouns from adjectives. Discovering a regular morphological feature of this type will enable us to make certain predictions when we encounter other forms in the language. For example, if the Kanuri word for 'length' is n mkurugu, then we can be reasonably sure that 'long' is kurugu.*
>
> *(Yule, 1996, 80)*

This shows us a vivid example in how the morphology knowledge is applied in language learning. Although I know little about Kanuri, I can easily understand this example. It is the morphology knowledge that tells us how to analyze and understand the word composition even in a totally strange language. It is the morphology knowledge that makes it much easier for the learner to remember a large amount of vocabulary, just like minimizing the quantity of the words by geminations.

Here I'd like to take Chinese language as an example to push this point further. When mentions that an estimated amount of 6170 languages in the world could be described by the knowledge of morphology, Jensen said that,

> *Some languages, such as Chinese, appear to have only simple words and compounds, and therefore very little morphology. Such languages have been termed* ***isolating*** *(Sapir, 1921).*
>
> *(Jensen, 1990: 2)*

According to my knowledge about Chinese characters, this statement does not seem so absolutely sound. Chinese is not that type of language which is composed of letters like English and most of the western languages. But we also have something in grammar like morphology, It is called 詞法, which means the grammar of word. And also something like morphemes, we call them 偏旁部首. In China, we have an old saying regarding the knowledge of words, if you do not know this word, just judge its meaning according to part of it and pronounce it according to the other part. 偏旁部首 in Chinese, is not exactly the equivalent of morphemes. But for the sake of convenience, I'd like to call them 'Chinese morphemes' here. These Chinese morphemes, some bear the meaning of the word and some carry the pronunciation of the word.

For example, 詞，means 'word', can be divided into two parts, 言 and 司. 言 indicates some of the meaning of 'word', means about word. 司 has something to do with the pronunciation of 詞. It pronounces similar as 詞. Another word 論, means 'discuss', is also formed by two parts, 言 and 侖, 言 is about word and 侖 pronounces the same as 論.

In Chinese characters, there are many ways of the creation of words. Examples I'd like to address here is one of them. This kind of characters are called 形聲字, means the word composed of two parts which indicate meaning and pronunciation of this word respectively. These parts, most of them can be independent words themselves and have their own meanings and pronunciations. These kinds of words are just like morphemes. They help to create millions and thousands of Chinese characters and help us to learn and remember and make a good use of Chinese language.

All of my students are Chinese. Since they possess the basic understanding of Chinese words morphology, it is not difficult for them to comprehend English morphology. Although different languages have their own characteristics and their own ways, they really share common similarities in many aspects.

My own teaching experience has proved that morphology knowledge is very useful in language teaching class. I remember that when we came across the word 'assistance', I explained this word by dividing it into morphemes assist+ance. 'Assist' is a verb, here in this word works as a free morpheme. '-ance' is a derivational bound morpheme, usually changes the part of speech of a word (usually a verb) into a noun. The students have known the meaning of the verb 'assist'; it is easy for them to remember what 'assistance' is. Furthermore, I brought up the word 'resistance' at that time. I asked one of the students what 'resistance' is. He knew the word 'resist' is a verb which means to counteract, stand against. And 'resistance' is the noun form of 'resist'. As the rule works, when they encounter the new words like acceptance, attendance, it is very possible for them to get the correct meaning and understand them within the context. There is a Chinese saying, a rule from one instance can be applied to three cases (舉一反三)(Here "three cases" means some more cases that the rule can be applied to, rather than the exact number). The practice mentioned above is an exact example for this saying. And it embodies the great significance of morphology in English language teaching. Let's take a look at how it helps in the learning of a long word. A long word is often comparably more difficult for the learner to remember and even to make a good use of it than a word which contains fewer letters. For example, helpfulness may seem a fairly long word for a beginner. But it is not difficult to learn when you break it down into parts according to the knowledge of morphology. '—ful' is a derivational bound morphemes which changes a verb into adjective form. And '-ness' is also a derivational bound morpheme which changes an adjective into a noun. 'Help' is an easy verb to learn. So the learner could get to the conclusion that 'helpfulness' is the noun form of 'helpful'. And 'helpful' is the adjective form of 'help'. Here morphology works to divide a long word into several parts which are comparably easy for the learner to understand and remember.

Part IV Take a Focused View on Prefix and Suffix

Prefix and suffix are typical kinds of morphemes in English language and form most of the derivational bound morphemes.

> *In the preceding group of words, it should be obvious that some affixes have to be added to the beginning of a word (e. g. un-). These are called prefixes. The other affix forms are added to the end of the word (e. g. -ish) and are called suffixes. All English words formed by this derivational process use either prefixes or suffixes, or both. Thus, mislead has a prefix, disrespectful has both a prefix and a suffix, and foolishness has two suffixes.*
>
> *(Yule, 1996: 69)*

This paragraph gives us a general concept regarding English prefix and suffix. Prefix and suffix work a lot in word formation in English. It is impossible to ignore them in English learning and teaching.

For example, the word 'prefix' has a prefix 'pre' which

means before. For this, we get the meaning of the word 'prefix' is that sort of affix which occurs before the word. When the students knows the meaning of this prefix 'pre', it is possible for them to make sense of these word, predetermine, prejudge, prearrange, predict and so forth. All of them indicate the meaning of before something.

For the suffix, take-ful as an example. When we are learning the word hopeful, I told the students that-ful is a suffix which changes a verb into an adjective. And then gave some verbs for them to change into adjectives, help, care, use, etc. They got the word helpful, careful and useful.

Of course, it cannot always work like this without any effort. It is not only the suffix '-ful' that can change a verb into an adjective. There are still some other suffixes which have the same grammatical effect. And each of them fits to different cases. So do the prefixes. The knowledge of morphology only offers a scientific means of learning the English words easier and better. To master all of them, the students need to learn more, read more and do a hard work to make it.

Part V How Does Morphology Work in Language Learning and Teaching?

As a study of word formation, morphology serves a basic learning skill in English language acquisition process, especially in English class. I remember that as a beginner in English, the basic grammar I was taught was concerned with third person singular present, past tense, progressive, past participle, plural, possessive, comparative and superlative forms. These eight forms are the all bound inflectional morphemes in English language. As described,

English Inflectional Morphemes		***Examples***
-s	*third person singular present*	*She wait-s at home.*
-ed	past tense	She wait-ed at home.
-ing	*progressive*	*She is eat-ing the donut.*
-en	*past participle*	*Mary has eat-en the donuts.*
-s	*plural*	*She ate the donut-s.*
-'s	*possessive*	*Disa's hair is short.*
-er	*comparative*	*Disa has short-er hair than Karin.*
-est	*superlative*	*Disa has the short-est hair.*

(Fromkin, 1998: 91)

In China, it is the most basic grammar and the first grammar which is taught to English learners. Although we have not mentioned the concept of 'morphology' when we know these rules, it is really morphology knowledge that we are learning. Only when we have mastered these rules, can we understand and perform an appropriate English. From this point, we could say that morphology is very significant and useful in English learning and teaching. Besides these basic rules, morphology works in English learning and teaching almost in every aspect. Let's take the four skills in language to see how morphology helps.

a) In reading skills

In English language learning, there are always a lot of work to do in readings, from intensive readings which focus on every details of the text to extensive readings which contains a large amount of information.

Intensive reading is a usual practice we are doing in English class. I have talked a little about this during the third part of this chapter and here I'd like to put more emphasis on extensive reading and especially on the exam module of skimming reading.

It is not surprising when an English learner finds that there are so many new words in an extensive reading text. In this case, it is not always a good idea to consult all of them from dictionary. When I was a student, I make a good use of word guess and find it a very practical method and I strongly recommend it to my students for their extensive reading. The basic idea of this kind of guess is to make full use of the ground knowledge to try to make sense of the new things. When encounter with a new word, just to guess its meaning from its form. To see if there is something familiar to you and what the meaning it is. At the same time, try to judge the part of speech of this word according to this sort of derivational morpheme. Here I'd like to take the concept of 'root morpheme', which often contains the main meaning of the word:

> *Lexical content morphemes that cannot be analyzed into smaller parts are called root morphemes.*
>
> *(Fromkin, 1998: 97)*

If you know what the 'root morpheme' means and you judge out what part of speech it is, you have figured out the meaning of the whole word. And then apply it to the context, you would get the exact meaning of it. This can be a very successful word guess. It is morphology that helps here. What about the case when it is impossible to know the meaning of the 'root morpheme'? Sometimes you still can have a good guess. At least, it is possible to make sure of its part of speech and this decides its function in the sentence. And then, it is possible to judge whether it conveys a positive meaning or negative meaning according to some morphemes like dis- unim- in- if there does have. This is of great assistance in understanding the word and the whole sentence, and then from the context to try to make sense of this new word. It is not always exact in practice, but sometimes in extensive reading, we do not always demand the conciseness of every word. It is just ok if you have made a near guess and get the whole concept of the text you are reading. It saves your time and do not prevent you from getting a large number of information. Of course, if you have time, it should be the best to look it up and make sure of its meaning. In this process of guessing and looking it up, your knowledge of the English language are perfected gradually.

This kind of word guess is especially feasible in exams which have a time limit and dictionaries are usually prohibited. In China, extensive reading which is called Reading Comprehension constitutes one of the English test modules. This module often contains about four considerably long texts for reading or skimming if you like. They are followed with some questions, blank fillings, True or False tellings and choice makings. It is similar with the reading module of IELTS test. I have sat IELTS once. What impressed me the most is that the reading task is of a huge amount. It is almost impossible to read and understand all the materials for even only once. Of course there are a lot of new words for me. It is a terrible experience because compared with the huge amount of the materials, the time seems so limited. In this case, what I could do with the new words is just guess. This kind of guess is certainly not a random guess. Unconsciously, I use the knowledge of morphology to help with it.

b) In listening skills

In language learning and teaching, the four basic skills never can be separated absolutely. In listening skills, morphology works similarly as in reading. But listening still has apparent differences from reading. Reading material is comparatively settled. The text is just there for you to refer to for as any times as you like, except for readings in exams. It is easy to turn to the dictionary for an understanding of a certain word. But listening is usually a one-time practice. When you hear something, it is more important to grasp its general concept in a whole instantly rather than to pay attention to every particular word. In this case, the 'word guess' seems much more important for the comprehension of the listening material.

The process of how to guess the word meaning with the knowledge of morphology is similar with that in reading skills.

c) In writing skills

The mental grammar of the language that is internalized by the language learner includes a lexicon listing all the morphemes and the derived words of the language. The morphological rules of the grammar permit speakers to use and understand the morphemes and words in forming and understanding sentences, and in forming and understanding new words.

(Fromkin, 1998: 95)

As part of grammar, morphology provides language learner a rule in word formation to follow. With a good knowledge of morphology, the language learner would be easy to choose and use the right and proper words in his/her writing in the target language.

d) In speaking skills

In speaking skills, morphology knowledge helps the similar as in writing skills. A big difference is that speaking is much more random than writing. There would be less time for the speaker to consider and less chance to modify. But morphology knowledge inside, as is described as *the mental grammar of the language that is internalized by the language learner (Fromkin, 1998: 95)* would work internally to correct and perfect his/her speaking skill gradually.

I remember that when I asked one of my students, what did you do yesterday afternoon? He replied, I go swimming. And corrected at once, oh, I am sorry, I went swimming yesterday afternoon. He knew that past tense for the verb should be applied here to correspond with 'yesterday afternoon'. But in speaking process, with no second thought, he said 'go' instead of 'went'. The morphology knowledge inside reminded him of this mistake and he corrected it immediately. I noticed that thereafter he performed much better in the employment of the past tense. Making mistakes and making corrections is part of the process of language learning. Within which, morphology and other grammar are working consciously or unconsciously to help the learner to perfect his/her language skills step by step.

Part IV Take a Focused View on Exceptions of Morphology

As all rules have their exceptions, morphology does not always work in the absolutely same way.

For example, we know that the inflectional bound morpheme '-s' helps to make a plural form, as As 'books' is the plural form of 'book'. Having known this rule, it is easy for a beginner to get the word 'sheeps' for the plural expression of 'sheep'. There is no word of 'sheeps' in English language. It is just still 'sheep', the same form and pronunciation as the singular form. And 'mans' are obviously unacceptable in English. Instead of adding the inflectional morphemes '-s', plural form for 'man' is 'men', a change of the vowel.

Another inflectional bound morpheme '-ed' indicates past tense of a verb. But 'eated' , 'goed' and 'hitted' inflected from this rule are all wrong words for the past tense of 'eat', 'go' and 'hit'. They should be 'ate', 'went' and 'hit'.

For these exceptions stated above, it seems that there are no rules to be summed up. Language learning is really very different from other sciences such as mathematics and chemistry. Rules do help but do not help all the time. In language learning, the old saying of no pains no gains is exactly validated. When one of my English teachers told me how to learn English well, she said, read more, listen more, write more and speak more. I believe in it and advice my student with it.

Part VII Conclusion

The study of word formation and the internal structure of words is called morphology. Part of one's linguistic competence includes knowledge of the language's morphology-the morphemes, words, their pronunciation, their meanings, and how they are combined. Morphemes combine according to the morphological rules of the language. A word consists of one or more morphemes. ...

(Fromkin, 1998: 97)

Morphology is the study of the rules of word formation of languages. With these rules, we are able to guess the meaning of the words that we've never encountered. Although it is true that this kind of guess is not always so exactly accurate, it offers an effective method in language study. This is very useful in English language learning and teaching. Realizing and making a good use of the morphology knowledge in English language teaching could help to achieve a lot.

Chapter Six

Teacher's Role in Classroom Discourse

Part I Introduction

People go to school to improve themselves by learning in various aspects for different purposes. Cazden says that the basic purpose of school is achieved through communication (Cazden, 2001:2). Whereas, the general concept *communication* is accomplished by everyday classroom discourses. Thus, class discourse has attracted lots of interests from quite a few expert educators. The study of classroom discourse is the study of that communication system (Cazden, 2001:2). By this communication, teacher helps students to cover what is called ZPD by Vygotsky,

> *The distance between the actual developmental level as determined by independent problem-solving and the level of potential development as determined through problem-solving under adult (teacher's) guidance or in collaboration with more capable peers (Vygotsky quoted in Alexander, 2000:431).*

Arguably the most important goal of education is change within each student that we call learning (Cazden, 2001:2). Here I would like to argue that the students are the principle part in a learning process. Meanwhile, teacher acts as a facilitator to help students in this cognitive process. With the power balance of individual to group, it is the teacher who is taking charge of the structure, pace and process of a class. The teacher's project is to complete the objectives on her/his agenda and to do so in an orderly way (Mehan, 1979: 82). In classroom, the teacher is responsible for controlling all the talk that occurs while class is officially in session—controlling not just negatively, as a traffic officer does to avoid collisions, but also positively, to enhance the purposes of education (Cazden, 2001:2).

Although there are the comparison phrases of *teacher-dominated* and *students-centred*, I agree with Alexander that the teacher's authority is unquestioned in the class. Whereas, this authority can be exercised in different ways (Alexander, 2000: 521).

Here the *different ways* depend on different specific class situations: the nature of the class, the set objectives on teacher's agenda, the class size, the student's background and so forth. Class discourse forms differ from one to another. No matter how different they are, the purpose of the class is to enhance students' learning to the possible maximum extent. The teacher plays a key role in this interactional cognitive process. To further this point, Alexander proceeds to say,

In any event, in the matter of making and keeping classroom talk dialogic, structured and enquiring, rather than loosely conversational, the responsibility is surely the teacher's.

(Alexander, 2000: 522)

Sinclair and Coulthard differentiate three key main kinds of classroom discourse: telling or expounding ('informative'), asking questions ('elicitation') and commanding ('directive') (quoted in Alexander, 2000:433). This comes accorded with what I think of the functions regarding the role of a teacher, information transmission (informative), scaffolding (mainly by elicitation, i. e. interaction with students) and class control (directive). How to perform these three functions well determines how much and how well the class academic goals are met with.

Centred on these three main points, in this essay, I will take a transcript of excerpted discourse from an English international language class to analyze the performance of the teacher and students, to see how a teacher acts in this particular class.

Part II Literature Review on the Topic

In the cognitive process, classroom discourse acts to accomplish most of the goals of learning. As Bakhtin indicates that truth is not born nor is it to be found inside the head of an individual person. It is born between people collectively searching for truth, in the process of their dialogic interaction (Bakhtin, 1984: 110 quoted in Skidmore, 2000: 293). Whereas, Classroom discourse differs from 'normal' conversation in that it is dominated by an exchange structure in which one party consistently both controls and evaluates the exchanges of the other (Alexander, 2000:433). This shows that teacher plays the core role in a classroom activity. Teacher's performance stretches a profound impact on students' learning effectiveness.

Wood indicates the significance of a teacher's role by saying that what distinguishes man as a species is not only his capacity for learning, but for teaching as well (Wood et al. , 1976: 89).

As I have mentioned in Part 1, teachers basically carry

out three functions in classroom discourse. These three functions interweaved with and interact each other in practice. By the scaffolding process, teacher achieves her/his academic purpose, which is transmitting knowledge to students. However, since a class is a sort of special social organization, it needs administration at the same time. To put emphasis on the controlling function of a teacher, Alexander says that a teacher's role is interventive rather than merely facilitative (Alexander, 2000:432).

Confucius, one of the greatest ancient educators of China says that the teacher's task is to transmit knowledge to students and help students to solve problems. This embraces the idea of scaffolding in teaching and learning process.

> *Scaffolding is the intervention of a tutor 'involves a kind of scaffolding process' that enables a child or novice to solve a problem, carry out a task or achieve a goal which would be beyond his unassisted efforts. '*
>
> *(Wood et al. 1976 quoted in educational discourse taught session).*

According to handout of the educational discourse session, scaffolding process involves the following aspects: recruitment, reduction in degrees of freedom, direction maintenance, marking critical features, frustration control and demonstration.

As for the issue of teacher's role, Cazden raises several

questions,

> *How do the words spoken in classrooms affect this learning? How does the observable classroom discourse affect the unobservable thinking of each of the students, and thereby the nature of what they learn?*
>
> *(Cazden, 2001: 2)*

Besides the basic functions mentioned above, how to exert proper skills to cater for different purposes of the class is a challenge for teachers.

What I would like to point out at the end part of the literature view is that I found that almost all the books I have read is concerned with the classroom talk dealing with children. It seems to imply that adult classroom tend to produce fewer verbal exchanges. In some cases, it is true. For example, many of the university classes are delivered in a module of lecture in which the lecturer does most of the talk to accomplish the information transmission function. I would like to argue that perhaps it is under such an assumption that adults are more capable in self-cognition than children and need less scaffolding and controlling from the teacher. However, although the knowledge in these books which mainly deal with children classroom, the principles are likely to apply to the adult classroom discourse as well. So I change some of the original words of 'child' and 'pupil' in the literature reviewed to 'student' in the quotation of this essay.

Another point I would like to make is that most of the relevant books use the concept of 'classroom discourse'. Thus, in this essay, I use 'classroom discourse' and 'educational discourse' interchangeably.

Part III Brief Introduction of the Sample Taken in This Essay

To record the sample discourse, firstly I think about taking it in China classroom. However, there are several drawbacks of this. Due to the inconvenience of distance and communication, it is not easy to do a fieldwork and get some first-handed information. Additionally, it is difficult to take the recording more than once to choose a more appropriate one for this essay. Another problem is that to do with the language. If I spot a Chinese-speaking class, the work of translation would be inevitably involved. I do not mind the extra work this will bring into this assignment. But the translation process will undoubtedly sacrifice some original information which might be important for the analysis. If select an English-speaking class in China to avoid the translation distortion, it is not easy to obtain a naturally-sounded effect.

It is fortunate that one of my classmates' friends is teaching in an international language school in Bath. She has been teaching English language in an international context for 5 years. She is willing to help me with this task after my explanation of my purpose. I went with her to the class to record for one time. Because I was there, she and the students felt a little nervous. She told me that she could hear her own voice sounded unnaturally. She is so kindly to offer to record another lesson without my presence. She gave me the recorded tape and it really sounds much more natural.

It is a 90 minutes recording involving the whole lesson. The main topic is about interview. The class process is interweaved by the activities of thinking time, writing down notes, discussing in groups and teacher's instruction. The transcript of 34 lines I take into this essay is mainly of teacher's instruction. By asking about the feelings of going to interview, she is trying to elicit a set of words which express certain feelings.

Altogether, there are 9 students in this class, 4 from Japan, 2 from Korea, 2 from Italy and 1 from Taiwan. Three of them are men and 6 of them are women. Their age ranges from 38 to 18. Pseudonyms are used here to protect their privacy.

The next part is a transcript of the excerpt I choose to contribute in this essay. I use a modified version of the conventions set forth by silverman (1997) quoted in Skidmore (2000),

[	simultaneous speech
[...]	omitted speech

(.)	pause of one second or longer
=	'latched' utterances, with no silence between them
No.	bold font indicates speech which is louder than the surrounding discourse (typically, where the speaker is emphasizing a point)
#Oh yeah#	degree symbols surround speech which is lower in volume than the surrounding discourse
(*laughs*)	italics within parentheses indicate contextual information interpolated by the transcriber

Part IV Class Discourse Sample Transcript

1. Teacher: [...]And so how did (.) or how did most you feel when you went to your interview? What kind of adjectives were coming now? I'll list here. *(pointing to the blackboard)*

2. Frank: Anxious.

3. Teacher: Ok *(writing down the word on the blackboard)* ok, what's another word for anxious?

4. Mike: nervous.

5. Teacher: Ok *(writing down the word nervous on the blackboard)*, and another one?

6. Frank: Shy.

7. Teacher: [Erm, shy doesn't mean the same as nervous.

8. Frank: [(hesitate)#Tim, tim, dyer...#

9. Teacher: Which word? What's it?

10. Frank: Like shy.

11. Teacher: Timid.

12. Frank: Timid.

13. Teacher: Erm, they are similar. Shy and (.) timid,

similar. *(writing down the word on the blackboard at the same time)*. But they are not the same as nervous. What's another word for nervous?

14. Frank: #Excevaded? Excevaded?#*(hesitating)(gives a non- English word perhaps influenced by his L1, Italian)*.

15. Teacher: #Excevaded? #

16. Frank: When you are excevaded…

17. Teacher: Excited?

18. Frank: Excited.

19. Teacher: **Excited.**

20. Teacher: Erm (.) again, it's not the quite, it's not the same meaning as these. Erm, Kate, can you have this word, another word for anxious or, or nervous?

21. Kate: #Erm…#

22. Teacher: The word begins with W.

23. Kate: #Erm, worried. #

24. Students: [Oh, worried.]

25. Teacher: [Worried. *(writing down the word on the black board)* Worried. Ok. You might be excited as well, and (.) not exactly the same meaning as anxious and nervous. But you might be (.) anxious in an excited way. =

26. Frank: That is a **mixed**…

27. Teacher: Yeah, a mixture. Yeah, so it might be a bit of mixture. You might be shy, and, or timid, timid is similar to shy.

28. Frank: Concentrated?

29. Teacher: erm…

30. Mike: #Interested?#

31. Teacher: You, you can't feel concentrated, you can't feel that, but you might have to concentrate, this is how would you behave, your behaviour, so you would concentrate, concentrate on the **questions**. *(writing down the word on the blackboard)*

32. Frank: #Ok. #

33. Mike: Interested.

34. Teacher: Yeah, that's a good word as well. *(writing down the word on the blackboard)*

Part V Analysis and Evaluation of the Sample Transcript

This is an excerpt taken from a language learning class from an international school. This sequence of classroom discourse bares the feature of responsive script introduced by Gutierrez (1994), within which there are several correct answers. The implied goals are a combination of getting the correct answer and developing shared understanding. This mode of discourse denotes increased opportunities for more students to participate in discussion (Gutierrez, 1994: 343).

In the 34 lines of exchange, 17 of them are of the teacher's, occupying exactly half of this discourse process. Teacher's words generally tend to be longer than students' contributions. I would like to argue that this is a teacher-dominated case centred on the language cognitive process of the students. Most of the students' responses are just one word as in lines 2, 4, 6, 12, 18, 21, 23, 28, 30, 32, 33. This is related with the specific aim of this class episode, i. e. , to tell the words indicating feelings in interview. By doing this task, the teacher is trying to elicit relevant words from students and share these with the whole class for a vocabulary practice.

This sequence has a clear pattern of what is called IRE, initiation-response-evaluation introduced by quite a few books. However, I prefer to use the concept of IRF here in this essay (Alexander, 2000: 433, Edwards et al. , 1995: 9). Instead of 'evaluation', he uses the word 'feedback' or 'follow-up'. From my point of view, there is a slight difference between 'feedback' and 'evaluation'. 'Evaluation' conveys more of the sense of a clear judgment. However, 'feedback' is relatively a neutral word which indicates a more widely meaning in replying to an answer beyond only an evaluation. In responding to what pupils say they use confirmations, rejections, repetitions, elaborations and reformulations (Alexander, 2000: 436).

It could be an interrogative sentence regarding the previous answer to make it clear to be understood, that is, to reformulate it, as in line 9. When Frank can not utter the correct word he is thinking about with an ambiguous remembrance of this word, he says in a hesitation in line 8, 'tim, tim, dyer…' It is a rather vague expression. Instead of ignoring his trying, the teacher helps him to reach the right answer by asking 'which word? What's it?' This is a feedback or follow-up rather than an evaluation of the student's answer.

Then Frank changes his strategy by explaining the meaning of the word he wanted to come up with as showed in line 10, 'like shy. ' It is an interesting phenomenon that some argue that in many traditional class the students are trying to guess what the teacher is thinking and try to play a gamesmanship (Alexander, 2000). But here it is the teacher who is guessing what the student is thinking by asking questions and understanding student's explanation to reach the right word in line 11, 'timid. ' In line 12, instead of the teacher, the follow-up role is played by Frank, saying 'timid' to confirm that it is the very word he was thought about. In this guess process, I think that the teacher does a very good job in scaffolding Frank's thinking. Whereas, Frank shows the ability of communicative competence mentioned by Alexander (2000: 457), i. e. answering well as much as answering correctly. He is not afraid of giving the wrong answer or even half-answer (he himself can not get to the right word he is thinking about) in his endeavour of contributing to the class discourse. I would like to argue that it is the style of the teacher's teaching that offers a way that students are able to address them with some degree of confidence (Alexander, 2000: 458). By this bilateral discourse (TIB pattern introduced by Kumpulainen), teacher and Frank work together to succeed in a joint meaning making (Kumpulainen) in this task and realize the moment of handover (Alexander, 2000: 430). We can find another good example in this transcript for this point. Line 14-19, the teacher helps Frank with the word 'excited' which he can not pronounce exactly. She shows a great patience in this interaction besides the very vague utterance of 'excevaded' from Frank in trying to guess what he is really driving at. Eventually, she reaches the correct word 'excited' with the confirmation from Frank in line 19.

To get back to the issue of the IRF I mentioned at the beginning of the previous paragraph, hereby I would like to say something about the first step, initiation. It can be noticed that teacher's questions have a good proportion in this discourse sequence. At their best, teacher's questions can both assist and assess student learning (Cazden, 2001: 92). This statement from Cazden implies that questioning forms a vital part in teacher's role of scaffolding. What to ask? How to ask? The skills of initiating questions have a heavy impact on the whole teaching and learning process.

As this discourse is a responsive script, most of the questions initiated are half-open, or use the concept of authentic questions which function as genuine invitations to the pupils to explain their views (Skidmore, 2000: 291) in comparison with test-like questions. The teacher is trying to elicit words expressing feelings in interviews. This defines a scope of the nature of the words: adjective, denoting feelings, etc. It is possible that teacher has a set of presumed words on her mind when she initiates this question. But she is willing to accept all the likely answers from students. In the course of this interaction episode, to get a proper (rather than correct) answer from students, the teacher uses both direct elicitations and cue elicitations (Alexander, 2000: 436). Cue elicitation is the teacher asks questions while simultaneously providing heavy clues to the information required (Alexander, 2000: 436). Alexander goes on arguing that the intention behind the cue is to scaffold. There are quite a few evidences of cue elicitations in this transcript. In line 22, the teacher gives the first letter of her expected words for Kate when she get into trouble in giving an answer as showed in line 21 and succeeds in eliciting the very word 'worried' eventually in line 23.

Elicitation skills is an issue which is worth of noticing. Mehan has introduced two forms of elicitations: repeating elicitations and simplifying elicitations. In line 15, the teacher repeats Frank's inaccurate utterance of 'exceveded', this is a simplifying elicitation, in which the teacher doesn't evaluate the reply while repeating the elicitation to the same or a different student, until s/he received a correct reply (Mehan, 1979: 56). In this transcript, teacher does an extra work other than what Mehan mentions, that is, to guess. In line 20 and 22, the example of simplifying elicitations can be spotted, in which the teacher simplifies elicitations when she does not receive replies to her elicitation acts (Mehan, 1979: 59). All these endeavour are made to meet the goal of scaffolding the student's learning by reducing the degree of freedom for the learner and accentuating critical features of the task (Mercer, 1992; Mercer, 1994; Wood et al. , 1976; Wood & Wood, 1996 in Skidmore, 2000: 288).

It is easily to be noticed that it is not only the teacher who is giving the feedback, but also the students are involved in doing this as showed in line 12, 18, 24, 32. In line 12 and 18, Frank repeats what the teacher says to confirm the teacher's guess. In Line 24 and 32, the students respond to teacher to show that they have understood the point what the teacher is trying to make. I would like to say that this kind of feedback indicates a positive sign in a classroom discourse to smooth and enhance the process of teaching and learning. As it has been pointed out that the effective teacher must have at least two theoretical models to which s/he must attend. One is of the task or problem and how it may be completed. The other is of the performance characteristics of the students (Educational Discourse taught session).

Another prominent feature I appreciate a great deal is the skill of 'uptake' in which the teacher incorporates a student idea into the flow of the discussion (Skidmore, 2003: 51). Good examples can be spotted in lines 25, 27 and 31. Although the students contribute words that are not eligible for the demands, the teacher takes up and makes sense of these words by developing and constructing them to her framework rather than rejecting them. For example, in line 31, she clarifies that you can not feel concentrated, but you should be concentrate on the (interview) questions. By doing this, she avoids discouraging the students' contributions and maintains the topic direction at the same time. From my point of view, what's important is that by taking up the unexpected words and explaining them to the whole class, she achieved extra results in teaching beyond her planned agenda for this class.

After some discussion about the teacher's two main functions: information transmission and scaffolding, I would like to talk about the class control role related with the turn-taking process in the class. As a whole, I appreciate what the teacher has done in her scaffolding effort to hand over information to students. But I do not think she has done a perfect job in the respect of turn-taking.

In this sequence, teacher seldom bids the turns by direct nomination (as she does once in line 20 by asking Kate) and the students select themselves to respond to the questions. There are 9 students in the class but only 3 of them speak in this sequence, i. e. , Frank, Mike and Kate. In the student's contributions, Frank does most of them which can be counted to be over 70 percent of all the students' proportion. I think that it should be better if the teacher offers more opportunity for other students' by raising more nominations. As Alexander points out that teachers should as far as possible equalize the distribution of their attention among all students, a strategy which raised the stakes in the processes of bidding, nominating and turn taking for willing and unwilling students alike (Alexander, 2000: 525). Additionally, handling turns by mutual consent is much more difficult than giving control of them to one person (Alexander, 2000: 472). There is a dilemma here that the methods for managing turn-taking reduce the likelihood of direct student-to-student exchanges (Skidmore, 2003: 51). Alexander also agrees that the teacher's task of steering a course between freedom and constraint is not always easy (Alexander, 2000: 522).

Despite these difficulties, I would like to recommend that it should be better if the teacher intervenes more to maintain a more equal allocation of turn-taking in the class.

Part VI Conclusion

Education is a form of communication (Barnes, 1992: 14). Verbal interaction between teacher and students are a form of communication which is perceived as educational discourse. I would like to argue that a study focusing on educational discourse is a study on specific methods and efficiency of class education in nature.

Almost all of us have practiced or are practicing the role of students or teachers. Barnes points out that perhaps classroom discourse has become invisible knowledge because we take it for granted (Barnes, 1992: 12). For a study on this issue, we should see the classroom discourse with an outsider's eye but an insider's knowledge (Barnes, 1992: 13).

In this essay, by introducing a small sequence of a piece of classroom discourse from an international language learning school and analyzing it from the views of a teacher's role, I am trying to explore how to exert a teacher's role to enhancing student's cognitive process.

The whole class lasts for 90 minutes and it is only possible for me to pick up one short episode. I can not say how typical this class is and to how much generalization this analysis could achieve. Since there are still other activities in this class set by different aims and launched in different modes and styles by the direction of the teacher and the joint working of everyone in the class. As Alexander indicates that every exchange has a history, or as Mercer suggestively has it, is part of a 'long conversation' (Alexander, 2000: 438). Yet micro cultures do not exist, cannot exist, in a vacuum: micro presupposes macro (Alexander, 2000: 436). A piece of discourse is possible to reflect some features which could apply to the general study more or less.

Centred on the three main functions of a teacher which I have mentioned in the introduction part, putting emphasis on the scaffolding process, in Part 5 I did a small analysis and evaluation of the transcript displayed in Part 4 on the basis of an literature review showed in Part 2. As a whole, I myself appreciate the teacher's performance in this episode. Whereas, it seems that she does not take much control on turn-taking process. For this, I think it is because the students are adult rather than children. If the intervention is not conducted appropriate enough, there will be the risk of some face-losing of some students, especially those active and talkative ones.

Classroom activities are organized to deal with specific goals on the teacher's agenda (Mehan, 1979:81). Teachers often plan specific script in advance to cater for specific goals.

According to the difference of subject, specific goal, class size and such other factors, class varies from class. It is not easy to say which mode is the most efficient method in enhancing the process of cognition.

After analysis and evaluation, I would like to argue that for all of the study on the educational issue; it seems not possible to reach to a perfect solution. Since the issue itself is a complicated one and what's more, the education itself is always on its way of developing and changing. Nevertheless, teacher's role in education is undoubtedly of great significance. What we can do is try to find out and carry out the most appropriate strategy for classroom discourse to meet various objectives of each specific class. Here I agree with Young that the point is that teachers should be aware of the alternative discourse patterns, and that they should critically evaluate the pattern they are using and the alternatives in terms of their educational value and introduce alternatives where it is valuable and feasible to do so (Young, 1991: 108).

REFERENCES

Alexander, R. (2000) *Cultural Pedagogy: International Comparisons in Primary Education*. Oxford: Blackwell Publishers.

Amin, A. & Thrift, N. (1995) 'Territoriality in the Global Political Economy', *Nordisk Samhallsgeografisk Tidskrift*, 20, 3-16.

Apple, M. (1979) *Ideology and Curriculum*. New York: Routledge.

Apple, M. (1982) *Education and Power*. New York: Routledge.

Assessment Reform Group (1999) *Assessment for Learning: Beyond the Black Box*. Cambridge, University of Cambridge, School of Education.

Bakhtin, M. M. (1984) *Problems of Dostoevsky's Poetics* (edited and translated by C. Emerson with an introduction by W. C. Booth). Manchester: Manchester University Press.

Barnes, D. et al. (1992) *From Communication to Curriculum*. 2nd ed. Boynton/Cook Publishers, Heinemann,

Porsmouth, NH.

Bassey, M. (1981) 'Pedagogic Research: on the relative merits of search for generalization and study of single events'. *Oxford Review of Education*, 7(1), 73-93.

Bell, J. (1991) *Doing Your Research Project: A Guide for First-Time Researchers in* Education and Social Science. Buckingham: Open University Press.

Bloom, J. , Hastings. T. & G. F. Madaus (1971) *Handbook on Formative and Summative Evaluation of Student Learning*. New York: McGraw-Hill.

Boulding, E. (1988) *Building a Global Civic Culture*. New York: Teachers College Press, Columbia University.

Bourdiew, P. & J. C. Passeron. (1977) *Reproduction in Education, Society and Culture*. London: Sage.

Broadfoot, P. M. (1996) *Education, Assessment and Society: A Sociological Analysis*. Buckingham: Open University Press.

Brown, G. & Yule, G. (1983). *Teaching the Spoken Language*. Cambridge: Cambridge University Press.

Burbules, N. C. & C. A. Torres. eds. (2000) *Globalization and Education: Critical Perspective*. London: Routledge.

Butterfield, S. (1995) *Educational Objectives and National Assessment*. Buckingham: Open University Press.

Bygate, M. (1991). *Speaking*. Walton Street, Oxford: Oxford University Press.

Capella, J. (2000) 'Globalization, a fading citizenship' in Burbules, N. C. & C. A. Torres. *Globalization and Education: Critical Perspective*. London: Routledge.

Carpenter, E. & M. Mcluhan. eds. (1970) *Explorations in Communication*. London: Cape.

Cazden, C. B. (2001) *Classroom Discourse: the language of teaching and learning*. Portsmouth, NH: Heinemann.

Cogan, J. J. (2000) 'Citizenship Education for the 21st Century: Setting the Context' in Cogan, J. J. & R. Derricott. eds. , *Citizenship for the 21st Century: an International Perspective on Education*. London: Kogan Page Limited.

Cogan, J. J. & R. Derricott. (2000) *Citizenship for the 21st Century: an International Perspective on Education*. London: Kogan Page Limited.

Cohen, J. (1989) 'Deliberation and Democratic Legitimacy', in Hamlin, A. & P. Pettit. eds. , *The Good Polity*. Blackwell, Oxford.

Cohen, L. & L. Manion. (1989) *Research Methods in Education*, 2nd edn. London: Routledge.

Commission on Global Governance (1995) *Our Global Neighbourhood*. New York: Oxford University Press.

Delanty, G. (2000) *Citizenship in a Global Age: Society, Culture, Politics*. Buckingham: Open University Press.

Dore, R. (1997) *'The Argument of the Diploma Disease: a Summary' Assessment in Education: Principles, Policy &*

Practice, Vol. 4, No. 1, 23-32. Carfax Publishing Company.

Dore, R. (1997) *'Reflections on the Diploma Disease Twenty Years Later', Assessment in Education: Principles, Policy & Practice,* Vol. 4, No. 1, 189-206. Carfax Publishing Company.

Drache, D. (1996) 'From Keynes to K-Mart: competitiveness in a corporate age', in Boyer, R. & D. Drache. eds. , *States Against Markets: The Limits of Globalization.* London: Routlege.

Edwards, D. & N. Mercer. (1995) *Common Knowledge: the development of understanding in the classroom.* London: Routledge.

Ellis, R. (1999) *The Study of Second Language Acquisition.* Shanghai: Shanghai Foreign Language Education Press.

Falk, R. (1994) 'The Making of Global Citizenship', in Bart van Steenbergen ed. , *the Condition of Citizenship.* London: Sage.

Feng, X. ed. (2004) Belgium Children Learn to Manage Their Money in *Qilu Evening News*, A6, 6 July 2004. Jinan: Dazhong Huatai Press.

Feng, X. ed. (2004) Anecdote of Chinese and American Education in *Qilu Evening News*, A6, 28 June 2004. Jinan: Dazhong Huatai Press.

Fromkin, V. & R. Rodman. (1998) *An Introduction to*

Language. Harcourt Brace College Publishers.

Gass, M. S. & A. Mackey. (2001) Data Elicitation for Second and Foreign Language Reasearch. Beijing: Foreign Language Teaching and Research Press.

Giddens, A. (2000) 'Citizenship Education in the Global Era' in Pearce, N. & Hallgarten, J. eds. *Tomorrow's Citizens: Critical Debates in Citizenship and Education*. Southampton, Institute for Public Policy Research.

Gipps, C. & G. Stobart. (1990) *Assessment: A Teachers' Guide to the Issues*. London: Hodder & Stoughton.

Gorard, S. (2001) *Quantitative Methods in Educational Research: the role of numbers made easy*. London: Continuum.

Great Chinese Educational Encyclopaedia (1985) *Educational Chapter*. Great Chinese Encyclopaedia Publishing Company.

Green, A. (1997) *Education, Globalization and the Nation State*. Basingstoke: Macmillan Press Ltd.

Grice, H. P. (1975) *Logic and Conversation*. In: Cole, P. & J. Morgan: *Syntax and semantics*. New York: Academic Press.

Gutierrez, K. D. (1994) How Talk, Context, and Script Shape Contexts for Learning: A Cross-Case Comparison of Journal Sharing *Linguistics and Education*. 5, pp. 335-365.

Hatch, E. & C. Brown. (2001) *Vocabulary, Semantics and Language Education.* Beijing: Foreign Language Teaching and Research Press.

He, B. (2001) The Experiment of General Senior Middle School New Curriculum and the Reform of National University Entrance Examination. In National Curriculum Committee Secretariat ed. (2001) *Research and Reform of Chinese Curriculum in 21st Century.* Beijing: People Education Publishing Company.

Heater, D. (1990) *Citizenship: The Civic Ideal in World History*. London: Longman.

Heath, S. B. (1983) *Ways with Words: language, life, and work in communities and classrooms*. Cambridge: Cambridge University Press.

Hedge, T. (2002) *Teaching and Learning in the Language Classroom.* Shanghai: Shanghai Foreign Language Education Press.

Held, D. (1991) 'Democracy and the Global System' in Held, D. ed. *Political Theory Today*. Cambridge: Polity: 197-235.

Held, D. (1995) *Democracy and the Global Order: From the Modern State to Cosmopolitan Governance*. Stanford: Stanford University Press. http://www. sdzs. gov. cn/policy/gaokao/2004/04031002. shtm accessed on 17 July 2004.

Hu, Y. eds. (2013) *Business English Writing*. Beijing: Foreign Language Teaching and Research Press.

Hu, Z. & Li, F. & J. Zhang, eds. (2000) *Modern Pedagogy*. Bejing: Higher Education Publishing Company.

Ichilov, O. (1998) 'Conclusion: The Challenge of Citizenship Education in a Changing World' in Ichilov, O. ed. *Citizenship and Citizenship Education in a Changing World*. London: The Woburn Press.

Ichilov, O. (1998) 'Patterns of Citizenship in a Changing World' in Ichilov, O. ed. *Citizenship and Citizenship Education in a Changing World*. London: The Woburn Press.

Isin, E. E. & P. K. Wood. (1999) *Citizenship & Identity*. London: SAGE Publications.

Janowitz, M. (1983) *The Reconstruction of Patriotism: Education for Civic Consciousness*. Chicago: The University of Chicago Press.

Jensen, T. J. (1990) *Morphology, Word Structure in Generative Grammar*. Amsterdam: John Benjamins Publishing Company.

Jiang, B. (2004) It is Difficult to Employ a Senior Technician for CNY5000 per Month in *Life Daily*, A3, 18 March 2004. Jinan: Dazhong Huatai Press.

Jiang, S. (2001) *Theory of Curriculum Reform*. Shijiazhuang: Hebei Education Publishing Company.

Kerlinger, F. N. (1970) *Foundations of Behavioral Research.* New York: Holt, Rinehart and Winston.

Kumpulainen, K. & M. Kovalainen. *The Discursive Practice of Participation in an Elementary Classroom Community.*

Kuo, I-C. (2006). Addressing the Issue of Teaching English as a Lingua Franca. *ELT Journal* 60. 3, 213-220.

Lawton, D. (2000) 'Overview: Citizenship Education in Context' in Lawton D. & Cairns, J. & Gardener, R. eds. *Education for Citizenship*. Continuum: London and New York.

Leech, N. Geoffrey. (1983) *Principles of Pragmatics*. London: Longman Group Limited.

Leedy, P. D. (1989) *Practical Research: Planning and Design,* 3rd ed. London: Collier Macmillan.

Lewin, K. (1997) 'The Sea of Items Returns to China: backwash, selection and the diploma disease revisited', *Assessment in Education: Principles, Policy & Practice,* Vol. 4, No. 1, 137-159. Carfax Publishing Company.

Lister, I. (1998) 'Citizenship and Citizenship Education in Britain' in Ichilov, O. ed. *Citizenship and Citizenship Education in a Changing World.* London: The Woburn Press.

Little, A. W. (1997) 'The Diploma Disease Twenty Years on: an introduction', *Assessment in Education: Principles,*

Policy & Practice, Vol. 4, No. 1, 5-21. Carfax Publishing Company.

Lowe, J. (2003) *Notes for a Taught Session of Assessment of Pupil Achievement*, MA Programme of Education Department, University of Bath.

Marshall, T. H. (1977) *Class, Citizenship and Social Development*. Chicago: University of Chicago Press.

Marshall, T. H. (1981) *The Right to Welfare and Other Essays*. London: Heinemann.

Marshall, T. H. (1992) *Citizenship and Social Class*. London: Pluto.

Mathew, D. (1996) 'Reviewing and Previewing Civics', in Parker, W. C. ed. *Educating the Democratic Mind*. Albany: State University of New York Press.

McNiff, J. et al. (2003) *You and Your Action Research Project*, 2nd edn. London: Routledge Falmer.

Mehan, H. (1979) *Learning Lessons: social organization in the classroom*. Cambridge, MA: Harvard University Press.

Miller, D. (1993) 'Deliberative Democracy and Social Choice', in Held, D. ed. , *Prospects for Democracy*. Standford: Standford University Press.

Mlinar, Z. (1992) *Globalization and Territorial Identities*. Aldershot: Avebury.

Munn, P. & E. Drever. (1999) *Using Questionnaires in*

Small-Scale Research: a Teacher's Guide. Practitioner MiniPaper 6.

Nattinger, J. R. & J. S. DeCarrico. (2000) *Lexical Phrases and Language Teaching*. Shanghai: Shanghai Foreign Language Education Press.

Palmer, F. (1983) *Grammar*. London: Penguin (Ch 3: Morphemes).

Passin, H. (1979) Review of 'The Diploma Disease' Pacific Affairs, 52(2), *Summer*, pp. 319-320.

Pearce, N. & J. Hallgarten. 'Introduction' in Pearce, N. & J. Hallgarten. eds. (2000) *Tomorrow's Citizens: Critical Debates in Citizenship and Education*. Southampton, Institute for Public Policy Research.

Porter, A. (1996) 'The aims of education for citizenship', in Lo, L. N. K. and Man Si-wai eds. , *Moral and Civic Education* (pp. 1-11). Hong Kong: Hong Kong Institute of Educational Research.

Poulson, L. & M. Wallace. eds. (2003) *Learning to Read Critically in Educational Leadership & Management*. London: SAGE Publications.

Pratte, R. (1988) *The Civic Imperative*. New York: Teachers College Press, Columbia University.

Proposal of the Improvement of the Educational Structure (2004) http://www. cas. ac. cn/html/dir/2004/03/03/1855. htm accessed on 18 July 2004.

Punch, K. F. (2001) *Introduction to Social Research: Quantitative & Qualitative Approaches*. London: SAGE Publications.

Ramphal, S. (1991) *Our Country the Planet: Forging a partnership for survival*. Washington, DC: Island Press.

Read, J. (2000) *Assessing Vocabulary*. Cambridge: Cambridge University Press.

Research Group of Curriculum Reform ed. (2003) *New Curriculum and Assessment Reform*. Beijing: Education and Science Publishing Company.

Robertson, R. (1992) *Globalization: Social Theory and Global Culture*. London: Sage.

Saeed, J. I. (2000) *Semantics*. Beijing: Foreign Language Teaching and Research Press.

Sapir, E. (1921) *Language: An Introduction to the Study of Speech*. New York: Harcourt, Brace, and World.

Sassen, S. (1996) 'Whose City Is It? Globalization and the Formation of New Claims', *Public Culture*, 8, 205-223.

SEC (1993) *Outline for the Reform and Development of Education in China* (Beijing, State Education Commission).

Skehan, P. (1999) *A Cognitive Approach to Language Learning*. Shanghai: Shanghai Foreign Language Education Press.

Skidmore, D. (2000) From Pedagogical Dialogue to

Dialogical Pedagogy. *Language and Education*. Vol. 14, No. 4, pp. 283-296.

Skidmore, D. et al. (2003) Teacher-Pupil Dialogue in the Guided Reading Session. *Reading literacy and language*. pp. 47-53, Blackwell Publishing Ltd.

Silverman, D. (ed.) (1997) *Qualitative Research: Theory, Method and Practice*. London: Sage.

Sinclair, J. McH. and R. M. Coulthard. (1992) 'Towards an Analysis of Discourse', in M. Coulthard (ed.) *Advances in Spoken Discourse Analysis*, pp. 1-34. London: Routledge.

Snyders, G. (1976) *Ecole, Class, et lutte des classes*. Paris: Les Presses Universitaires de France.

Su, Z. (2004) *Epidemic of Chinese Education*. Yancheng Publishing Limited Company.

Tou, (21 March 2004) *Chinese Imperial Examination*. http://www. yourblog. org/Data/20043/24001. html accessed on 14 Jul. 2004.

Tribble, C. (1997). *Writing*. Great Clarendon Street, Oxford: Oxford University Press.

Vygotsky, L. S. (1978) *Mind in Society*. Cambridge, MA: Harvard University Press.

Walliman, N. (2001) *Your Research Project: a step-by-step guide for the first-time researcher*. London: SAGE Publications.

Waters, M. (2001) *Globalization* 2nd ed. London: Routledge.

Whitty, G. (1985) *Sociology and School Knowledge: Curriculum theory, research and politics.* London: Methuen.

Widdowson, H. G. (1989) Knowledge of Language and Ability for Use. *Applied Linguistics.* Vol. 10, pp. 133-134.

Wikipedia, the free encyclopedia. *Synonym.* https://en. wikipedia. org/wiki/Synonym accessed on 11 June 2017.

Wood, D. et al. (1976) The Role of Tutoring in Problem Solving Child Psychol. *Psychiat.* , Vol. 17 pp. 89-100. Great Britain: Pergamon Press.

World Commission on Environment and Development (1987) *Our Common Future.* New York: Oxford University Press.

Xie, Y. eds. (2013) *Commercial English.* Beijing: University of International Business and Economics Press.

Yeates, N. (2001) *Globalization & Social Policy.* London: SAGE Publications.

Young, R. (1992) *Critical Theory and Classroom Talk.* Clevedon: Multilingual Matters LTD.

Yule, G. (1996) *The Study of Language* 2nd ed. Trumpington Street, Cambridge: University Press (Ch 8: Morphology).

Zhang, T. (2001) Curriculum Reform: the Process of Innovation and Inheriting. In National Curriculum

Committee Secretariat ed. (2001) Research and Reform of Chinese Curriculum in 21st Century. People Education Publishing Company: Beijing.

Appendix 1　Questionnaire

This questionnaire is given in both Chinese and English.

You can answer it in either language.

本次问卷中英对照，请根据个人喜好选择一种语言做答。

Questionnaire

调查问卷

Dear friends,

Now I intend to do a case study about the impact of National University Entrance Examination (NUEE) on your learning and life. Could you please fill out this questionnaire to help me in this research? This questionnaire is anonymous and will cause no negative effect for you.

Many thanks for your kindly attention and assistance.

同学你好，我现在需要进行一个关于高考及教育测试方面的调查，需要您协助填写这份问答卷。此次调查采取匿名形式，不会影响到任何人对你的看法。

Please tick the appropriate square for the choice items.

关于选择题，请在合适的方框内打对勾。

Gender 性别：Male 男□　　Female 女□

Age 年龄：________　　Date 填表日期：________

Part 1 第一部分

1. Why do you want to go to university?
你为什么想上大学？

2. What major would you like to study at university?
如果考上大学，你想选择什么专业？

3. What's your plan after graduation from University?
你大学毕业以后打算做什么？

4. What will you do if you fail the NUEE?
万一考不上大学，你有什么打算？

5. Are the tests results and ranks made public each time? If yes, what's your opinion about it?

你们测试的成绩和排名公开吗？如果公开，你对成绩和排名的公开有什么看法?

6. What are the most important things that you think you have gained from your schooling?

你认为你上学得到的最重要的东西是什么？

7. Have your teachers been teaching you exam skills? Do you think them useful?

老师有没有针对考试传授考试技巧？你觉得考试技巧有用吗？

8. Do you think it reasonable that the admission to university is determined by the result of NUEE? What other factors do you think should be counted in the university entrance selection process?

你认为用高考成绩决定大学入学的方法合理吗？你认为还有什么应该考虑在内的因素?

Part 2 第二部分

1. How important is NUEE to your life?

你认为高考在你的一生中很重要吗？

very important 非常重要□ important 重要□

indifferent 无所谓□ not important 不重要□

hard to tell 难说□

2. Are you confident in succeeding in the NUEE?

你有信心考上大学吗？

Yes 有□ No 没有□ hard to tell 难说□

3. Do you plan to take the NUEE again in case you fail it this year?

如果没有考上理想的学校，你打算明年再参加高考吗？

Yes 参加□ No 不参加□

4. Do you feel that your current study is intense?

你觉得现在的学习紧张吗？

extremely intense 非常紧张□

very intense 比较紧张□

fairly intense 还好□

somewhat not intense 不是很紧张□

not intense at all 很轻松□

5. Do you have mock exams for NUEE?

你们有高考模拟考试吗？

Yes 有□　　　　No 没有□

6. What is the frequency of mock exams?

模拟考试的频率是____________________

7. What do you feel about the frequency of mock exams?

你认为模拟考试的频率如何？

Too much 太多了□　　　　a little too much 有点多□

appropriate 正合适□　　　　a little less 有点少□

too less 太少了□

8. Do you think that mock exams are helpful?

你认为模拟考试有用吗？

Yes 有□　　　　No 没有□

9. Do you like exams?

你对考试有什么看法？

Yes 喜欢□　　　　No 不喜欢□

feel afraid of it 害怕□　　　　indifferent 无所谓□

10. How many hours do you spend on studying yesterday?

昨天你学习了几个小时？ ____________

11. What do you usually do at your leisure time?

除了学习你有什么课余活动？ ______________

Thanks again for your kindly cooperation. 感谢你填写本表。

NOTE:

A further interview based on this questionnaire is a significant part of the research. If you feel like to take part in a small interview which is just like a conversation carried on WeChat, please let me know by writing down your contact information here. Your kindly assistance will be greatly appreciated.

又及：非常欢迎你通过微信和我一起做一个关于高考和学习问题的访谈通话，如果你愿意参加，请在这里留下你的联系方式，谢谢。

Appendix 2 Interview Questions

1. Do you think that the knowledge you are now learning at school is useful and practical for your future career? If yes, to what kind of degree?

你认为现在学的知识对你以后的工作有实用性吗？

2. Do you think that the subjects which are examined for NUEE are rational? What other subjects do you think necessary to be taken?

你认为现在的高考科目设计合理吗？你认为还应该学习什么课程？

3. For the fourth question in the first part of the Questionnaire, some answer to go on with studying in case failing the NUEE, how and where to go on with studying?

调查问卷第一部分第四题，万一考不上大学，就争取另外上学的机会，都有什么机会？

4. For the fifth question in the first part of the Questionnaire, majority of the classmates answer that they accept the exam result made public, because it helps to know one's learning achievement and the difference from others.

Additionally, this helps positive competition and making progress. However, if you are free to choose whether the exam result being made public or not, what will you choose and why?

第一部分第五题，大多数同学赞成公开成绩，也习惯了，因为可以更好地了解自己，促进竞争和进步，如果学校让你选择，公开成绩和不公开成绩，你选什么？为什么？

5. For the eighth question in the first part of the Questionnaire, many classmates mentioned that the moral character, civism, and the ability in taking part in social activity should be taken into consideration for the university selection, do you agree with this and what do you think about it?

第一部分第八题，很多同学提到大学入学应该考虑到品德，公德心，参与社会活动的因素，你同意吗？

6. Have you taken citizenship education ever since and when? Do you think it necessary?

你上过公民课吗？你认为公民教育重要吗？

7. For the eighth question in the first part of the Questionnaire, some mentioned unifying the minimum entry score of the whole country, what do you think about this?

第一部分第八题，有些同学提到全国分数线统一的问题，你有什么看法？

8. For the eighth question in the first part of the Questionnaire, some mentioned to add an entry interview into the university entrance selection process, what do you think about this?

第一部分第八题，有些同学提到大学入学增加面试的

问题，你有什么看法？

9. For the eighth question in the first part of the Questionnaire, some mentioned to cancel all of the bonus score, what do you think about this?

第一部分第八题，有些同学提到取消一切加分奖励的问题，你有什么看法？

10. For the eighth question in the first part of the Questionnaire, some mentioned to take the daily performance in school into consideration in the process of university entrance selection other than the sheer one-off NUEE, what do you think about this?

第一部分第八题，有些同学提到要把平时在学校的表现考虑在内的问题，你有什么看法？

11. Could you please talk more about what do you think about the examination skills?

能不能深入谈谈你对考试技巧的看法？

12. Do you think that examination can really improve your learning and why?

你认为考试可以促进学习吗？为什么？

13. Do you think that the diploma is of the utmost importance for your life?

你认为文凭对你来说是最重要的吗？

14. About NUEE and mock exams, what else do you like to comment?

关于高考和高考模拟测试，还有一些有关高考的问题，你还有什么其他想法？